SECONDS
AND INCHES
A MEMOIR

BY CARLY ISRAEL

D1603714

Published by Jaded Ibis Press.

www.jadedibispress.com

 JADED IBIS PRESS

Thank you to my family and friends. You know who you are, and you are loved. And to the four men who own my heart. I live and die for you.

In memory of Alexis, Mitchel & Kayleigh . . .

"For a seed to achieve its greatest expression, it must come completely undone. The shell cracks, its insides come out and everything changes. To someone who doesn't understand growth, it would look like complete destruction."

-Cynthia Occelli

"The trouble is, you think you have time."

-Buddha

CONTENTS

Part Three:
The Fire   211

FOREWORD

These are the words.

"I got you": These are the words I (try to) live by. These are the words I had tattooed on my left inner forearm in Nashville while I was visiting a woman who had lost a child, a woman I had given a scholarship to for one of my retreats to France. These are the words I whisper to myself like someone possessed with a weirdo inner self-help guru. For the record, I whisper them incessantly to drown out what I call the IA (Inner Asshole), which tells me exactly the opposite: *No one has you. You are all alone.*

When I read *Seconds and Inches*, Carly Israel's haunting and beautiful memoir, these are the same words I felt. "I got you." There they were again. This time, they were within the pages of a book—a book that wasn't mine but could have been. The journey was that reminiscent, that similar, that universal. Carly's story is not simply hers. It belongs to many of us.

It is the story of *not* dying when you thought you might, when you *really* wanted to. It is the story of letting go of the belief that you are a garbage person, not worth a damn, and accepting that you are indeed not a garbage person; you are capable of deep love, and you are, despite what your IA has told you quite often, enough.

However, it wasn't my memoir. It was Carly Israel's. And yet, that is what a good book does. It makes you keep closing the book to check out the cover and make sure it isn't your name on the cover because you relate so much. It has to be your story. There is no way someone got inside your head and wrote this.

But she did. And it serves as a reminder that we are all human. The details are always different, of course. The family history in *Seconds and Inches* is fascinating, and layered, and not the same family history as anyone else's who reads it. And yet, it reminds us how easy it is to carry pain and trauma from one generation to the next, how loss is unavoidable, how being what I call a Human Thank-You is the only way to find meaning in life.

I always say this is my mission statement: "When I get to the end of my life and I ask one final 'What have I done?' Let my answer be, 'I have done love.'" People often ask what that means. What does doing love look like? Now, I have this memoir I can give them, the one in your hands (or e-reader, let's be honest), and I can say, "Here is your roadmap on what doing love looks like. Here is your guide."

This isn't a book about overcoming anything. Carly talks about addiction, and loss, and having a child with a mysterious medical condition, and divorce. (There's more, but I don't want to spoil it, so I will let you find out for yourself.) But she does not overcome anything. She finds herself. She finds God (often in the most unlikely places), and she finds new eyes. Which is to say, she begins to look at everything through the lens of gratitude.

This is not a how-to book, and you will not finish the last page and know how to win at life. What you will want to do is write a thank-you letter to everyone you know, including your past self. You will want to go out and live fully. You will want to stop hiding and accept your imperfect, perfect self. You will want to start telling the truth about who you are.

What else could you ask for in a book?

-Jen Pastiloff

* * *

Jen Pastiloff travels the world with her unique workshop "On Being Human," a hybrid of yoga related movement, writing, sharing out loud, letting the snot fly, and the occasional dance party. Cheryl Strayed, author of *Wild*, calls Jen "a conduit of awakenings." Jen has been featured on *Good Morning America*, *New York Magazine*, *Health Magazine*, *CBS News* and more for her unique style of teaching, which she has taught to thousands of women in sold-out workshops all over the world.

She is also the founder of the online magazine *The Manifest-Station*. Jen leads annual retreats to Italy and France and she is the guest speaker at Canyon Ranch and Miraval Resorts a couple times each year. She also leads Writing and The Body workshops with author Lidia Yuknavitch.

Her memoir, *On Being Human*, was a national best seller. She has created a massive online following from her personal essays and teachings. Follow Jen on instagram at @jenpastiloff or Facebook at Jennifer Pastiloff. She is also the creator of @nobullshitmotherhood and @gPowerYouAreEnough on instagram. Her motto to live by is Don't Be An Asshole. She even owns the URL.

DISCLOSURE

Some names have been changed to protect the privacy of individuals. I have done my absolute best to tell the stories of my ancestors and my own life based on stories told directly to me and from my memories. And while I know that this is said in all memoirs, I need to put it out there: Nothing has been made up, but some would argue that how I remember is not how they do. My intention is to tell my story with the hope of harming no one. This memoir is not intended as a substitute for the medical advice of physicians. The reader should regularly consult a physician in matters relating to their health and, particularly, with respect to any symptoms that may require diagnosis or medical attention.

INTRODUCTION

My last name, Israel, means one who wrestles with God. And wrestling is all I know. This story comes from a long line of God-wrestlers who have come within seconds and inches from life being completely different. I am a truth seeker and will always be looking for meaning, but what I have found, so far, has altered more lives than I can possibly count.

It started out with a daily commitment for one year. I had heard about Mark Zuckerberg's personal challenge to send a thank-you card to someone in his life every day for a year. I was intrigued but also knew I would never be able to accomplish that because my life is nonstop. I decided that I would publicly post a thank-you to someone every day for one year. I needed something that I could commit to but also something realistic. I needed to set myself up for success with this, taking into account that I have three boys, a job, a hubby in another state, and a handful of women I mentor. Posting on social media every morning was manageable.

I like placing myself in a position where I have to take action that will inevitably change me. The challenge was to post a daily thank-you note for a year to someone in my life (alive or dead, known or from afar) who has brightened my path. When I first started, I defined being brightened as being made happier by. And then it evolved to illuminating the darkness so I can see clearer. As I continued to write, my friends seemed to lean in towards thank-yous that came from hard or painful lessons. Like watching my son get bullied on the bus and having to keep it together all the way home until he burst through our door and lost it. Even in those moments, I had to find something to be grateful for.

What I discovered as I wrote my daily thank-yous was that we all want to be seen. To be heard. To mean something. My UPS driver, Jim, is one of the happiest humans I know. He was my thank-you one day, and I decided to share it with his manager and team, and I saw something shift in Jim. He felt known.

I received messages from readers who needed me to know that what I was sharing was also their own private truth, but they didn't have the wording or courage to share it themselves. Once I began to look for people to thank, I saw opportunities everywhere to let others know that they mattered, that their kindness made a difference, that I was changed because of something they did or gave.

And the thank-you process became contagious. It is a gift that is free and priceless. My boys—Franklin, Elijah, and Levi—have picked up on it, too. One day, when Levi needed to write an apology letter (for being a jerk) to his friend, he said, "I have to write," and then he stopped himself; "No, I get to write this letter." He's nine. So, practicing acknowledged gratitude is possible for us all.

Some of my thank-yous were intensely painful to write: to admit to making fun of the boy who overheard me doing it in high school and thanking him for teaching me to never do that to another human again. It became a regular occurrence to receive messages from people I hadn't seen in decades.

When I read these messages, I heard my inner voice guiding me to keep going. That if even one person was helped by me baring my insides, it was worth it. And as I opened my heart to these relative strangers, it gave them permission to do likewise.

People asked to know more about my story and how I got to a place where I was able to see gratitude in any situation. And because I was only showing them small glimpses, like quickly opening my towel to flash my naked body, it felt like it was time to let the towel drop and bare all.

At first, I was too afraid to open the attic packed with dusty trunks and overstuffed boxes full of stories I've been carrying around since before I ever set foot on this earth. These stories have come to me, tugging on my pant leg, pleading with that part of me that truly believes we are all connected. That believes we are all worthy of a witness who will acknowledge the meaning in what has happened to us. And in spite of all the metaphorical hallways I try to avoid, the universe always does its magic and brings me exactly to the right place, joining me with the people who will guide me to the next doorway.

I have found the courage to crack open the trunks within my soul and tell the stories of those who came before me. By connecting all of our stories, I was able to step far enough back to take in the whole. I saw generations who struggled with God. I even discovered a great-great-grandfather who, after emigrating from Germany to NYC at seventeen, joined Company A (a battalion known as the "Lost Children") while fighting in the Civil War and was then thrown into Andersonville Prison (one of the deadliest prisons in the country) after being captured by the South. While at Andersonville, he tried to escape twice while fleeing bullets that riddled his legs and bloodhounds that chased him back to his cell.

I realized that my ancestors, like myself, nearly escaped death on multiple occasions. I unburied the magic and strength of those who walked with me, taught me grit, and pushed me when I couldn't go on because they believed in something I didn't even know was in my heart. I found that I am not the only one in my lineage to survive by seconds and inches.

The question I asked myself at age nine—when I stared in the mirror at the golds, greens, browns, and blues of my eyes and knew I would be someone someday—is the same question I wrote in the black and white composition notebook I filled with my pain right before my attempt to end my life. It is the same question that has pressed me up against the wall as I matured and came back again as a mother, and a seeker, and a lover:

Who are you?

Maybe my whole life, I've been asking the wrong person. Maybe the answer can only be found when we're willing to go back far enough into our past and listen to the voices and whispers of those who are no longer here to speak. Maybe I needed to walk with the broken, frightened young woman who never had anyone to tell her that she was worth so much more than what she was settling for.

Maybe I needed to be for myself what I always wanted every guy to be. Maybe I needed to almost lose everything that meant anything in order to see the beauty and the wonder all around me. Maybe it wasn't only about looking into my past but also about unfolding into who I was meant to become. Maybe the answers could only be understood when I put all of the pieces together and then stepped far enough away to take it all in. Like an Impressionist painting, where the full depth and meaning can only be truly seen and appreciated as a whole.

If you asked me when I was twenty-five what the worst time of my life had been, I would have answered from my experiences with my alcoholic parents or from my own years of alcoholism and drug addiction. But I didn't know then that the worst was yet to come and that I would need every single thing I had walked through to make me strong enough to walk through that level of darkness. To find out my youngest child had a potentially fatal medical condition. To carry him through everything that came after.

Disconnected

There's not enough concealer in the world
to hide the dark circles under my eyes.
I walked too far.
I walked past too many doors
to the back, where only hospital personnel are admitted
and I saw too much.
I saw the bloodied rags left on the floor of operating rooms.
I saw things I wasn't supposed to see
and now I cannot unsee them.
I can never look at God in the same way,
with the same trust.
It's as if I sold my God for your life.
The question remains:
What if I'm not imagining any of this?
What then?
There's no one else holding you down while you scream.
I whisper in your ear, "Mama's here, Mama loves you."
How very alone I feel in caring for you.
My chest is tired and constricted.
This is not nothing.
There is something wrong
and once again
no one knows a thing.

Part One:
My Holocaust

Chapter 1:

Trapped in a Burning Building

I am locked inside a dark, disgusting room—a frat room or a crack house. Spilled bottles and garbage, ashtrays full of cigarettes, empty pizza boxes and styrofoam containers are everywhere. Glass bongs caked with soot. The smell of bong water and burning fabric coats my nose. There is loud bass music coming from the speaker, and the air is thick with smoke. The heat is stifling. I'm sitting on a filthy, stained couch with duct tape over the holes. I can hear the screaming sirens outside. The building is on fire, and I am locked inside this room.

The truth is, I put myself in this building and I shut myself in this room. I can hear the banging on the exit door at the very end of the hallway, but the firefighters can't get to me. The only way out of this room is to break open and climb out the small window in the door to the hallway and then wade through all the crap stored in there. I've packed the hallway with boxes and trash bags full of excuses, stories, sadness, and rage that keep me safe and isolated from everyone that can hurt me. I've barricaded myself in with my sob stories and fears and guilt and shame, and I refuse to let anyone in.

I wear a sash like a beauty queen except mine reads "Broken." I cannot see a way out. I will never be able to get out. I cannot hear God. God doesn't want anything to do with a girl like me. And never will.

Chapter 2:

Shtetls and Fox Holes

I come from many holocausts. Some during World War II, some with screaming sirens and flashing lights, and some in my childhood home on the suburban cul-de-sac of Diane Drive. I was born of these stories, and I carry them with me wherever I go. They burn within me, begging to be told.

Everything I know about my ancestors was told to me in pieces. We do not have a family tree. We can't trace our family back generations. There are hardly any pictures left. There are no family heirlooms. All I have are their stories. Stories told to me while I lay in Grandma Lulu's bed as she and I cut out coupons and she twisted my hair and tied it with a cloth. Stories whispered to me on an airplane trip across the country to California. Grandma Gerry's hushed memories shared while our tray tables held our ginger ales and peanuts, my mouth opening in disbelief, Papa Bernie in the row behind us pretending not to hear. The missing pieces falling into place. Learning why my dad freaks out when we play with matches or candles. Why Papa Harry never read any cards we gave him.

Both of my grandfathers were in the war, but only one received the triangle-folded flag at his funeral. I didn't know Papa Bernie had been a soldier until he died. He lived an entire life without ever talking about landing on Normandy, earning a Purple Heart, or losing so many friends. His generation came home in silence. Looking back, I remember the songs he would sing: "I had a girl, ten feet tall, slept in the kitchen with her feet in the hall. Sound off! Three, four."

Papa Bernie was only ten when his father died, so he had to grow up in a hurry. Grandma Gerry told me all I know of Papa Bernie's mother, saying that her husband's mother was "certifiably crazy, constantly seeing doctors, always in and out of the hospital. You know she's the reason Bernie never let any of us see a doctor for anything having to do with feelings."

While one grandfather was thrust into adulthood, the other was forced to live a life unimaginable to me. In a part of Poland that I can't pronounce, Papa Harry's family was evacuated from their home, confined and segregated into the cramped ghettos. There was my great-grandmother, Bracha, and my great-grandfather, Chaim (whose photos I have never seen), and their eight children. At some point, as rumors were circling under the Nazi regime and my family's inescapable fate was unfolding out of their control, a desperate plan was hatched. A plan that sometimes keeps me up at night when I allow myself to imagine the conversations between a mother and father with their eight children lying nearby, huddled together to keep warm. I can picture their whispers and disagreements. I can picture the uncertainty that must have plagued their every waking moment. Which one convinced the other?

From men in the village, Chaim had heard stories about where they were taking the Jews on the trains. Death was certain for all of them, he must have realized, and so he came up with a plan that would gamble the lives of his eight children. His plan would set off a chain reaction that eventually resulted in my life and the lives of my children. He was a terrified father, powerless to keep his family safe. And so, he threw a Hail Mary, the outcome of which he would not live to see.

The story goes: One night, Papa Harry's parents gathered him and his oldest four siblings, including his oldest brother, Teddy, oldest sister, Molly, Papa's twin sister, Sylvia, and their next-youngest sister, whose name I never knew. Papa Harry was only nine years old when he listened to his father's hushed instructions for each of them take a loaf of bread, climb over the ghetto wall, split up so no one would know the kids were together, and try to escape. Nine years old. My youngest is nine. He's allowed to walk three blocks max in our safe neighborhood to a friend's house.

How tightly did his mother hug her five oldest children? What did they say to each other in those final moments, knowing it was the last time they would ever hold them in their arms? How they must have kissed their foreheads and tried to capture their scents, crying, sick to their stomachs with worry, never to know if their decision would be the right one.

Bracha and Chaim would soon be forced to leave all of their possessions behind and board a stifling, packed train with their three remaining daughters: one hungry toddler and two crying babies. I imagine them as they stood in line at Treblinka, known as a true death factory, knowing that five of their children might escape their turn in the gas chambers because of a decision they made. I imagine a glimmer of hope in their otherwise terrified eyes.

As my great-grandfather was separated from his wife and three baby girls, told to strip naked, and beaten by the Nazis, I imagine him holding onto the only thing they didn't take from him: The belief that his plan for his older children would work. That plan would end up creating more than seventy heirs to his story. I don't think he was able to imagine that he would have a great-granddaughter who would one day attempt to share his courageous story with the world.

While Papa Harry was running through the night with the loaf under his arm, cheeks wet with tears, and abject terror in his mind, five-year-old Grandma Lulu was escaping the Nazis with her family on their horse and wagon. She would tell me these stories over and over because she, like me, is a storyteller and needed to get them out. But Papa Harry stayed silent. When I would ask him questions about that time, he would shake his head, cover his mouth with his big hand, and look off into the distance.

To my maternal great-grandparents, Chaim and Bracha,

There are no family pictures of you to share with my children. I have never seen what your faces looked like. When asked who I would like to have dinner with, alive or dead, I always choose you. I want to sit down with you for a few hours and listen to the story of how you made the decision no parent on earth wants to make. Somehow, you found the courage to gather your five oldest children and send them over the ghetto wall to an unknown fate. The pain and fear you must have felt when you hugged your children for the last time traps my breath in my chest. Zucha Lipe (Papa Harry), your second-oldest son, was nine. He was the same age as my youngest, whom Zucha had the pleasure of meeting on the other side of that wall, in a country you'd never been to, in a life you could never imagine him living. You made the right choice. I counted: seventy-three descendants resulted in that choice to send your five oldest children away from your arms. Four of the five survived. Hidden, alone and terrified, four of your

children lived. And I knew all of them. They were
mensches of the highest honor, good humans you'd
be proud of. Thank you for making a decision
I hope to never have to make. Thank you for
sacrificing your last days with your children in the
hope they could possibly survive. And survive they
did. Your legacy lives on.

Chapter 3:

Sylvia's Choice

What I know of the five siblings who got away makes my stomach burn. Teddy was captured immediately and sent to do forced labor. He built roads in the cold with his bare hands by day and was chained to a tree, like an animal, by night. Papa's twin sister, Sylvia, was blonde and blue-eyed and, therefore, able to hide in the home of a gentile family by working as their maid. Molly, the oldest, also hid and worked as a maid. Their youngest sister, whose name I never learned because none of the survivors dared speak it, was the least fortunate.

German soldiers caught her after they heard a drunken rant from one of the town prostitutes. The prostitute claimed there was a young Jewish girl working for a family in town, that the girl had a sister, and that she knew where to find both of them.

Sylvia had been scrubbing the breakfast dishes when the three Nazi soldiers barreled through the house. They demanded that she come with them, grabbing her by the arm and pulling her out of the house. Sylvia didn't know where they were taking her, but the soldiers' presence was causing a scene that attracted a crowd. The house she worked in was very close to the town center. As they rounded the corner, Sylvia saw a soldier holding a German service rifle, a K98

Mauser, pressed to the head of a skinny, blonde girl. Sylvia saw that the skinny, blonde girl was wearing the familiar work boots of her sister.

The SS soldiers held her little sister at gunpoint, and the others holding Sylvia laughed. One of them spit on the ground and shouted, "*Ist das deine Schwester?*" Is this your sister? Sylvia's sister did not look at her. She stood very still, trembling, almost imperceptibly, with the gun at her temple. Sylvia looked away.

The crowd grew bigger. People stared. Many of them wanted the Jews out of their country just as much as the Nazis did, if only because of all the trouble and commotion they were causing. Some stood by wanting to stop this madness, but they knew the price of sympathizing or intervening was their lives.

Sylvia was silent. She refused to look at her sister. Instead, she stared at the onlookers desperately, as though pleading for help. If she admitted the little girl held at gunpoint was her sister, they would both be killed. The soldier demanded again, "*Ist das deine Schwester?*"

Sylvia still didn't answer, and the soldier smacked her face. Sylvia looked at her sister, the rifle pressed to her head. The sun was shining down, and Sylvia saw four pigeons tearing apart a crust of bread. She heard them squawking, as though it were any normal day. Sylvia's sister was still and silent with a dead look in her eyes. Briefly, the two sisters locked eyes. Sylvia saw resignation there and something else: an unspoken absolution.

And, just like that, with a shake of her head, Sylvia said, "*Nein.*"

A deafening gunshot echoed through the square, and her little sister crumbled to the ground. The shot rang in Sylvia's ears; smoke wafted out of the end of the German rifle. The soldiers laughed and lit each other's cigars. One of them kicked her sister's lifeless body with his jackboot. And it was that kick that did it.

Sylvia felt something break and fall inside her. She knew then that an important part of her had died with her sister. The kick dislodged it, made it fall, and the emptiness left over was almost comforting. It's what allowed her to stand there, pretending not to care, and wait for the soldiers to leave, so she could return to the home where she worked. Sylvia would remain that empty shell, haunted by that decision forever after. The haunting manifested in physical pain. Later in life, she suffered gastrointestinal pain so severe that she could hardly eat. The sickness and the emptiness terrorized her until her last days.

Dear Sylvia,

Oh, Taunta Sylvia, you were one incredibly special woman. As I wrote about your childhood, I felt compelled to tell you how right you were about that decision you were forced to make when you were just a little girl. You were weighed down with guilt for what happened the day those Nazis made you choose between telling the truth and saving your own life. I can imagine what it did to you, living with that decision hanging around your neck your whole life. I know it made you physically sick. I know it made you mumble about that little girl even in your eighties. But, I need to tell you something: You made the right choice. Because of that unimaginable choice, you survived.

And with your survival came your children and your grandchildren, and they are all valuable and essential people. Your son helped me when I was struggling, and your grandson works with our family and is such an incredible man. Everyone loves him, with his Papa Harry-like looks and kind manner. And because of that choice you were forced to make, I am here. If it wasn't for you, Papa Harry and Lulu would never have met at the bakery by your apartment, and none of my family would be who they are today. Thank you for sharing your kind soul and generous heart. Your brave and impossible decision completely changed the world.

Chapter 4:

In the Woods

Papa Harry was originally taken in by a gentile farmer until word spread that the Germans were out searching homes for Jewish hideaways. The farmer then sent him away to hide in the forest behind his farm. The forest was at least a half mile from the edge of the farmer's barn. Before he sent Harry away from the safety of his house he whispered, "Wait until it is completely dark and then quietly come to the back of the barn. I will leave whatever I can for you to eat hidden in a milk crate."

Some nights, the milk crate was empty, and Harry had to make his way back with his growling stomach pains and hope that he could find or catch something to eat in the forest. The sounds of the forest were, by far, the hardest to endure. The howling of animals he could not see. The stomping of the Nazi boots when they did raids on the surrounding areas and sent their dogs into the forest to find hideaways like him.

He lay perfectly still, trying to hold his breath so he would be invisible and silent. Some nights, he dreamed of the last morning in his old home: the breakfast plates that were interrupted, jam on his mother's dish, and the spilled fresh milk across her linens.

Some nights, he would cry himself to sleep, wondering what happened to his sisters and brothers. Were they hiding like him? What about his parents and his little baby sisters? Papa Harry's father had told him before he left that he must never speak Yiddish, that he had to forget the language completely, in case someone heard him and turned him in. Even in his sleep, he had to dream in another language.

Harry lived on his own in the woods for two years. On the few occasions my papa spoke to us about his memories, he shared how he had to dig a hole where he hid and cover himself with sticks and leaves so the Nazis wouldn't find him on their searches. He told us how he fended off wild dogs by holding a stick in each hand: one to distract the dog and the other to hit the dog on the head. He was ten. My ten-year-old can barely distinguish the toaster from the microwave.

Papa Harry wore the same clothes, boots, and hat that he wore when he ran away. He had nothing left of his mother or father. Nothing to show for the life that was stolen from him. He told me once that he still had nightmares. That he could no longer remember what his mother's face looked like. Did it look like Sylvia's? Did it look like my mother's?

I wonder, as the Nazis separated men on one side and women on the other, if Papa Harry's parents had any hope left in their hearts for the five children they sent away. I cannot fathom that kind of pain, and love, and powerlessness. I cannot bear the heat of it in my body. If their decision to send away their older children wasn't made, if my great-grandparents naïvely believed that they would make it through if they only all stuck together, nothing would be as it is.

As Papa Harry was hiding in the cold, dark woods, my other grandfather was landing on the shores of Normandy with fears all his own. The only tangible proof I have that Papa Bernie was a soldier is the set of dog tags I wear around my neck—one of my most sacred items—and a single photo. I have a picture of him in his army training uniform, smiling with his arm around a fellow soldier, proud, and young, and ready to serve. We never became one of those military families with pride, and celebration, and honor. I know so little of what he experienced. He earned a Purple Heart and a Bronze Star Medal. He survived and never talked about it. I know that he grew up learning not to talk about painful experiences, and that was the best he could do. Sadly, not talking about hard times would, one day, destroy his family.

Grandma Lulu, Papa Harry's wife, is the great storyteller in our family. Much like myself, she is bursting with life and loves talking about the past. She was born in a *shtetl* in Poland and lived on a farm. She told me about surviving Tajikistan, Siberia, L'viv, and Poland while living in labor camps and learning six languages. She shared with me, "The main road was filled with neighbors running as bombs dropped all around us. I heard the older people praying and praying, and then a bomb would land nearby, and there was no more praying. Nobody explained what was happening." Not one member of her extended family survived. She explained that none of it—not the Holocaust, not the bombs falling from the skies on September 1st—none of it came close to the horror of growing up between the hatred of her parents.

Grandma Lulu leaned toward me, put her hand on my hand, and said, "The story of your great-grandparents is better than any soap opera." Years before Lulu was born, her parents caused gossip and drama with their love affair. She gazed at our overlapping hands as she spoke. "My father, Yitzhak, whom you are named for, was a soldier in Russia. He loved life, and danced on tables, and later became a tailor in a neighboring town. He was hired by a wealthy family, rich enough to hire a tailor to make their son's trousseau, that owned land."

She paused and looked up at me. "Do you know what a trousseau is?" I shook my head. "It is the clothing a bride gets tailored before their wedding, but because this family was so wealthy, the groom was having it made for his bride."

"The groom brought his younger sister, Gitel Baldinger, who spotted Yitzhak and fell in love with his good looks and sense of humor. Gitel wanted to marry Yitzhak, the young tailor, but her family refused to allow the marriage. Eventually, Gitel's misery wore her family down, and with her dowry, Yitzhak moved to Bobowa in Poland. The two married and had a son, Moishe, my brother."

"Soon after my brother was born, Yitzhak met my mother, Rivka, who, back then, was very beautiful, and the two fell in love." Lulu explained that the story did not end well because the whole village blamed Rivka for breaking up Yitzhak and Gitel's marriage.

Divorce and second marriages were unheard of at that time, and great controversy followed the new couple. Lulu whispered, as if someone from old-world Poland might overhear, "Gitel's family hired professional cursers—there was such a thing—to curse the second marriage, and Gitel died of a broken heart when Moishe was only nine months old. Her wealthy family would not allow Yitzhak near his own son. He was brokenhearted to be forced to leave his son. My mother, Rivka, brought a daughter of her own to the marriage. My parents had two children together, me and my other brother, Hymie."

But the love story doesn't continue from there. The two came to the new marriage with their own darkness, and they fought instead of communicated. Eventually, Rivka was never happy with anything Yitzhak did. The misery of her parents' marriage would haunt Lulu for decades. It would also be what linked the two of us in solidarity when my own marriage crumbled. Her empathy, as a child of divorce, would one day transform into open arms for me.

These are the thank-yous that rose out of my ancestors' ashes that molded me into the girl I became and the woman I am today.

Papa Harry,

The two of us had a special relationship—we fought all the time. We fought over gin rummy, how much food I was wasting, and what to watch on TV. You taught me the art of sarcasm from a very young age. When I would ask, "Where's my mom?" you would answer, "she ran away and left you," then smile for the imaginary audience. You taught me inappropriate Yiddish words, and you laughed a lot. You couldn't keep a secret, which is why they called you Loose Lips Gips. You were always in a rush to get life over with. You loved to offer me a pickle for a nickel. But what I am most thankful for is that you taught me, through your quiet example, that everyone has their own headaches and who are we to complain about ours? Your spirit is so missed here. When something bright gets into my eyes and makes me squint, I look around for you and feel a huge loss. Your great-grandchildren will know your story. Your children are mensches because of the

way you and Lulu raised them and because of the
man you were. Your wife has missed you and misses
you still. Please visit her in her dreams. Please
comfort her in her loneliness. We found a picture
you carried in your wallet of your bride when
she was in her early twenties. Sixty-four years of
marriage and no doubt that is how you still saw her
at the end. For you, we will wear our pants up high,
we will start the coffee as soon as the main course
is set down, we will bake challah, and we will teach
our babies about the courage you had and the man
you were. Not only am I a better human for having
you as my papa, but the world is a better place for
having you in it. *Guy cacan yamaran* (go poop in
the ocean).

Dear Lulu,

Everyone who has ever met you says the same
thing: "I love Lulu!" Your life is stories—volumes
upon volumes of all you've been through. You
speak six languages, can cook a whole Shabbat
dinner on the same day you're treated for breast
cancer, make bellboys escort our luggage from an
unacceptable hotel to the Plaza, and leave the ER
too soon after breaking your nose. (You broke it
when you fell trying to keep up with our power
walking on the mean, fast-paced streets of NYC,
only to return to the Diamond District to get
some earrings to distract you from your broken
nose.) You were willing to wear a disposable, paper
bathing suit in the hotel pool because your six-year-
old granddaughter begged you to come to swim

with her. Thank you for being the one to push
my parents to get sober. We needed you, and you
always showed up. And then I had the privilege
of helping you find your way to sobriety, and our
relationship got so much closer. Thank you for the
endless grocery store gift cards. Do you know how
I almost cry each time I use them and tell the clerk
that my grandma pays for our groceries? And I will
never forget the kindness you gave to me and the
example you were when I told you how my life was
falling apart. When I shared that I couldn't stay in
my marriage, you said right away that you were
not God and you would never judge me. And then
you told me about how horrible it was to grow up
in a family where the parents couldn't stand each
other. I want to respond like that anytime someone
opens up to me and is waiting to see if I will judge
them. But what I'm most grateful for is what
you did for our family: The relentless planning
and manipulating to get all of us together every
year. And it has paid off more than any round of
blackjack you played. You are the Godfather of our
family. I love you, and I thank you for your shining
example. Now put on a red sweater so you don't get
a *kenahora*.

Chapter 5:

The House on Channing

Papa Bernie, who came home a war hero and quietly hid away all medals and signs of military life, never to be discussed, was about to experience his own holocaust. Grandma Gerry had a whiskey laugh and green, sparkly eyes, both of which she passed on to me. Her hair color changed like the Cleveland weather as she went about mothering three young boys, one after another. First came Marc, then my father, Alan, and then, a few years later, their youngest son, Evan. Papa Bernie was a workaholic, and Grandma Gerry was a homemaker.

They lived at 2419 Channing Road in University Heights, Ohio, with their three boys and then, finally, a baby girl, Marcie. These were the days of fancy parties at the house, and drinks after work, and mothers in heels.

On the evening of December 24, 1959, Grandma Gerry was at her makeup table, hair in curlers, hors d'oeuvres in the oven, punch bowl on the buffet table. Ten-year-old Marc and eight-year-old Alan were at a sleepover, so they wouldn't be bored staying upstairs during the holiday party. I imagine five-year-old Evan and two-year-old Marcie were freshly bathed, in their footie pajamas, hair combed, and tucked into bed. They shared a room, with Evan's twin bed next to his world globe and Marcie's white wooden crib in the corner.

Bernie, an outgoing salesman, and Gerry, a social butterfly, loved to entertain, and the house was packed with friends and music and cigarette smoke and holiday cheer. The party went on just past midnight while their two youngest slept quietly in the room above the tar roof at the back of the house.

At 4:14 a.m., a neighbor walking his dog called the University Heights Fire Department. The report reads, "On arrival, found entire backroom den involved by fire and house completely charged with smoke. Raised ladder to the south wall of the back bedroom but could not make an entrance because of heat and smoke. Raised ladder to front bedroom to rescue man calling for help. In the process of getting on the ladder, he got on before ladder was set causing the ladder to fall sideways, carrying him with it. A woman jumped from other front bedroom window before our arrival. Two adults were taken to Suburban Hospital by police ambulance. Proceeded with the search for children behind 2½" and 1½" hose lines laid into the house and up the stairway to the second floor."

As Grandma Gerry told me on the plane ride to California, she and Papa Bernie woke to incredible heat and smoke in their master bedroom. Bernie sent Gerry out by the window while he went to rescue Evan and Marcie. It was later stated in the report that my papa was seen wandering the hallway, trying to get to his children, but was overcome by smoke and was in a confused state. He was found calling for help by the third-floor window. When the firefighters lined up their ladder, one of the metal hooks was not yet attached when Papa Bernie grabbed it and swung his body to escape the flames. The ladder fell backward and on top of his chest. He was found unconscious.

Grandma Gerry was seen shouting in her bathrobe at the neighbors below who were trying to alert the firemen that there were four children inside. Grandma Gerry explained to me that she kept shouting, "There's only two!" but no one believed her because the neighbors did not know that Marc and my father had slept out. During the commotion, she fell from the window and landed on the cement front steps, cracking her head open. She, too, was found unconscious, her body splayed in an unnatural position.

Chapter 6:

Big Brother

Gerry was somewhat of a spectacle in town with her three boys all lined up behind her at the grocery store and at the butcher. But when baby Marcie came, all the onlookers stopped asking her when she would go for the girl. She finally had her little girl.

Evan and Marcie were only two years apart. They roomed together, played together, and were often grouped together as the little kids. Evan took his role as Marcie's big brother very seriously, making sure she always had someone to catch her at the bottom of their slide and making sure she got a turn when the older brothers were playing in the yard. All of the boys were enamored of their little sister, but there was a special closeness between Evan and Marcie.

That evening, they were the only kids in the house. Their big brothers were sleeping out, and they were tucked into their beds and told to stay upstairs while Mommy and Daddy had their friends over. They could hear the laughter and music. They could smell cigarette smoke mixed with their mother's famous chocolate chip *mandel* bread. The two had fallen asleep well before the party had ended but were startled awake by the raging fire outside their bedroom window.

Marcie and Evan's room was directly above the addition with the new heater and recently tarred roof. Evan woke to Marcie's crying. Normally, he rolled over and plugged his ears because he knew his mommy was coming to get her before she woke the big brothers. But this time, something was different. There was heat and orange light, and their mommy never came. And Marcie's cries grew more frantic.

Evan pulled the striped covers back from his twin bed and crept, barefooted, to Marcie's white spindle crib. Her cries were frightening, and she was calling his name, "Evie, Evie, Evie," as she held onto the bars with her chubby two-year-old hands. He grabbed the bars on the side of her crib and put his little, naked feet in between each bar, so he could pull himself up and over the top. Marcie reached for her brother, and the two lay like spoons as Evan covered his ear with one hand and her outside ear with the other, to soften the roaring.

Evan couldn't find Marcie's milk bottle or her pacifier. He just held her and cried, "Mommy's coming. Mommy's coming," until they passed out together from the fumes and smoke.

When the firemen got to Evan and Marcie's room, they did not find anyone in the twin bed. The covers had been pulled back, but no child lay sleeping. They found the five-year-old boy with his baby sister in her crib. The report stated that the window of the bedroom where the two children were found was so hot that the firefighters could not approach it from the outside.

The Captain wrote in the incident report, "I responded to the alarm in Engine No. 1, with four firemen. As we turned onto Channing Road, I saw a red glow in the sky, traveling south on Channing Road. I thought the fire was in the house on the southeast corner of the intersection of Channing Road and Hillbrook Road. The house looked like it was burning from the first floor through the second floor."

There is one picture, in particular, in the file that was breathtakingly terrifying. It was of the zoomed-out view of the bedroom where Marcie and Evan were found. There is a white crib on the left, a nightstand and a twin bed on the right with striped covers pulled back. The window above the twin bed is broken. There is a firefighter standing in the middle of the room, holding a flashlight, staring at the crib. A dolly lies inside. There is a baby bottle on the floor under the crib. Did it fall while she was asleep? Did she get to drink all of her milk? The firefighter's profile is in shadow, and he is in uniform.

Both children were found unconscious, and their limp bodies were passed from fireman to fireman. There were two resuscitators on the fire trucks, and men worked on each little child as they laid them on the blankets set up on the driveway. There were two resuscitators, but only one worked that evening.

As fate would have it, Evan got the working one. "As a result of smoke inhalation, Marcie Israel, age two and a half years, was dead on arrival at the hospital. Evan Israel, age five, was confined in the hospital in serious condition. His parents, Bernard, age thirty-five, and Geraldine, age thirty-three, were confined in the hospital with bruises and smoke inhalation on Thursday, December 25, 1959."

Dear baby Marcie,

> We drive by your house on Channing often. My
> boys know your story, but I didn't learn about you
> until I was twelve, on a plane to California with

your parents to visit your brother, Evan. Your mom
whispered every detail into my ear. It all made so
much sense. Why my dad, your brother, Alan,
freaked out if we played with matches or fire or
candles. And I found out my original middle name
was chosen in your memory, but then they changed
it to Michelle instead of Marcie. Because Michelle
in Hebrew means life, and they didn't want me
to carry what you had to endure. Your mother,
my grandmother, told me she had to stop talking
about you because, after a while, people were so
uncomfortable with that depth of grief. She told
me certain days were so painful for her, like your
birthday and the anniversary of your death. She
told me everything. Since then, I've wondered if I
look like how you would have looked. Or what it
would have been like to have a biological aunt. But
I keep your story inside and carry it with everything
else that burns. I am so sorry you didn't get to live
a long life. I would have loved to know you. I am a
descendent of your story. And the universe whispers
to me sometimes to tell it. And I have, sweet baby
Marcie. You have made my life more awake.

Dear Evan,

I treasure the warm connection we had while you
were alive. You were a talented writer, but what you
were best at was being a father. I loved watching
you as a father. Those long vacations when I would
get to spend weeks at your house in Palm Desert,
watching you laugh, and tease, and gently love
your children in a way I hungered for from my
own father. It was attractive and memorable. When

I heard about your fatal glioblastoma diagnosis, I was crushed. Your death changed me. I was angry at God and felt so helpless. We talked about it, and you were loving and available for me as you were going through it all. Watching you get sick during the hell of clinical trials just to squeeze in a little more time with your family and watching you decline and struggle, it altered me. I think of you every time I'm stuck behind someone driving too slowly. Because you had to stop driving when you got too sick. As each of your freedoms was taken from you, it taught me to pause and remind myself to be grateful. And that maybe the person driving slow in front of me is also struggling. I'm grateful that you survived the fire and, at only five years old, you knew to climb into your baby sister's crib, so she wouldn't be alone. Thank you for all of the laughter and love you gave to this world. Your children have grown into wonderful and productive adults and parents. You must be so proud. I miss you so incredibly much.

Chapter 7:

Whispered Family Secrets

I do not know who told my grandparents that Marcie didn't survive. I do not know when my father and his brother were brought to the hospital. My uncle Evan would be in a coma for six months. Doctors did not know if he would survive. When he finally woke up, he had to learn how to walk and talk all over again.

Marcie's funeral and the tiny casket were arranged for the following Sunday. Only one member of the immediate Israel family attended: My father, then eight years old. I picture him in a little, dark suit. I worry about him because no one helped him through that trauma—he was sent to stay at friends' houses—and I wonder if anyone ever comforted him. He never went to therapy. They barely spoke of Marcie or the fire.

When the details were finally shared with me during that flight from Cleveland to California when I was twelve, I thought most about my dad. It came up when we were discussing my middle name, Michelle. Grandma Gerry explained that I was first named after Marcie, and I asked, "Who's Marcie?" I had no idea. After that trip to California, I had a new understanding of Grandma Gerry and my father. After the trip, she took me to her storage locker to show me newspaper clippings about the fire. The fire and the heat and the loss and the sympathy for my dad curled up and stayed in the space where my ancestors live: a burning house in the pit of my stomach.

It was three decades later when I knocked on the side door of the University Heights Fire Station and asked them if they had any records about that fire left. They told me that half of the records from that time were destroyed by water damage in the storage room but that they would check and get back to me.

A few hours later, I received a message that the records from my family's fire were intact and the file was thick and full of details that supported all I had shared with them. I was finally going to get more information. I had so little from my family, and there was no one left to answer my questions. I went back to the same firehouse that responded on that fatal night and found pictures, records, police reports, and descriptions that mirrored what Grandma Gerry had told me all those years before.

Where we come from changes us, whether we are aware of it or not. The heat and the weight of what our ancestors endured is passed on. Grandma Gerry asked me to write her story. When she was in her chemo chair, when I was older and a mother, she told me to tell the story and liberate myself from that burning-house past. I drove by that fire station for months, wanting to stop in and ask. But I waited until she died. I couldn't write about the worst night of her life while she was still here.

Almost every detail I relayed when I came asking for records was accurate except for the cause of the fire. We were always led to believe it was from a lit cigarette left burning by one of their guests. The real cause was from a little heater that had been left on in the addition on the back of the house. For almost sixty years, we all thought differently. Grandma Gerry's friends thought the same and would sometimes wonder if, maybe, it had been one of their cigarettes that did it.

Dear Papa Bernie,

I wish I could sit with you today, as the woman I am with so many questions and so much love to share. I can still hear your gritty cough as you struggled to breathe, and now, I wonder how much of your emphysema was from the cigarettes and how much was from the smoke inhalation and the fall off the ladder. What was it like to land on Normandy? Did you ever watch any movies about WWII, or did you deny those difficult memories in the same way you never spoke of the fire or Marcie? You were always kind to me. I remember your laughter and playing War with you at the kitchen table, your beefy arm with your rocks glass up in the air and your battle cry, "Hip, hip, hooray, we're having a party!" I think about the pain you must have experienced when you came to in the hospital after the fire. I want to thank you for being a mensch even after experiencing such darkness. You taught me the meaning of that word, and your great-grandsons, with your name intertwined in theirs, strive to be mensches just like you. Thank you for the memories, and thank you for serving our country. I wish you could have told me about those times, but I imagine if you could've told me, you would have. Your son, my father, the only one who went to Marcie's funeral, ended up very similar to you. He works a lot and takes care of his family, but, like you, he doesn't like to talk about painful memories. But know this, Papa, I am breaking that chain, and we are beginning to heal, and you would be proud of the mensch your son has become.

Dear Grandma Gerry,

I have many memories of you and us. I think of you every time I make *mandel* bread. I got my big, green eyes and whiskey cackle from you. Thank you for taking me to see all those plays at Heights, and teaching me to love theater, and showing me that gummy bears can make a bubble bath way more fun. Thank you for pretending you were a spy, so I wouldn't tell anyone that we had to pay one of your speeding tickets. Thank you for speaking to me again after I sent you that horrible letter with all of my angry words. Thank you for forgiving me after the years of not getting along. Thank you for loving me as I am. I come from really strong ancestors, you among them, and I get the strength that comes from honesty from you. Thank you for telling me about the fire and for trusting me with your story and your memories of Marcie. Thank you for treating me like an equal. You were wrong when you said I was going to have a difficult time finding a man who wants me with my three children. I found one just crazy enough, and you would love him. How did you survive burying two children? A most unnatural act for any parent. Your strength and endurance speak to your character. I cried so much more than I imagined I would when you died. I thought I was ready because you had been so sick for so long. But I wasn't ready, and I miss you still.

Chapter 8:

The Kids Are Not Alright

This fire burns within me. The forest where Papa Harry hid, Sylvia's choice to save herself and watch her sister die, Lulu's fear escaping those bombs, what private horrors Papa Bernie saw on those battlefields, the fire my father survived but lost his sister in—all of it and much more lives in my body, embedded in my DNA. These fathers before me—one sent to live alone in the woods, and my father, who stood at his sister's funeral and was then sent away to live with friends until Papa Bernie and the family figured out where to go next—I feel them moving my feet. These mothers before me, they beat inside my heart.

They were without help. They had no therapy. They had no coping tools. Each of my ancestors was traumatized during their formative years. Each had their own holocaust. I began to wonder how our children are affected by what we pass on to them and whether it shapes them into the people they are. A professor of mine once said, "If you are hurt, you will hurt," and these cycles will repeat if we don't repair what's broken. Maybe who I would become at their age was connected to who they were. I, too, was wandering and alone in the dark.

But before there was me, there was Alan and Beverly. That eight-year-old boy—who stood at his sister's funeral all alone, who never got help, and who grew up in a family where the fire and his sister were never spoken of again—he became a skinny, long-haired, bell-bottom jeans wearing hippie. And that hippie crashed the birthday party of a tow-headed, hair to her waist, first-generation Polish-American named Beverly. Men had just landed on the moon. The Beatles were taking over the world. And these two wandering souls found each other.

Alan and Beverly were inseparable from the start. They were often pictured holding hands and were married before her nineteenth birthday (with pink, rolled-up marijuana joints offered on their guest tables). He became a pharmacist and gained closer access to drugs. She raised their Great Danes, which she shoved into their tiny, red, VW Bug to visit home in Cleveland from Ada, Ohio. Onlookers in Ada would ask where their Jewish horns were. Because those Bible Belt people had never encountered Jews before, and they were told all Jews had horns. The two lived in a trailer with their baby boy, my brother, Adam, while my dad went to pharmacy school.

My mom wanted nothing more than to be a mother. But in those early days, as evidenced by most, if not all, pictures, her eyes were tiny, mascara-lined slits squinted at the camera, barely conscious from whatever concoction of pills and vodka she had consumed that night. There is a picture of her looking like that while leaning over to light the candles on my Big Bird birthday cake, and I wonder how she was capable of taking care of me in that state.

Much of my childhood was joyful. I wandered outside on Laurelhurst, laughing and running through the sprinklers and attending barbeques with family. There were Friday night dinners at Lulu and Papa Harry's with drinks and chocolate-covered everything. And at Grandma Gerry and Papa Bernie's, there were frequent parties where he lifted his thick arm, holding his ever-present rocks glass, to salute and bellow, "Hip, hip, hooray, we're having a party!" But along with the Z. Cavaricci pants, the mustache brushes, and the cocaine gold press-on pinkie nails, there was the heavy secret of the mornings after, when my mother cried in bed and my father made us hug her and tell her it would be okay.

The secret we were never to share with anyone, especially our grandma Lulu, was what was happening inside our house. No one could know that our mom was passed out drunk and high on the couch most days after work or that our dad drank all night after he got home. What I learned early on was to keep the outside looking good. Be well-dressed and well-behaved, and no one would know anything about what was going on inside.

One of my worst memories is from when I was five. I don't remember my mom tucking me in for the night, I don't remember what pj's I had on or what story we read, but I do remember waking up in the middle of the night on a very high bed in a strange, dark room that wasn't my own. When I got the nerve up to dangle my feet over the side of the bed until they hit the floor, I crept out of the room to where I heard voices and laughter. My dad appeared, picked me up, and put me back in the high bed. I could smell the boozy heat of him, and it made me go rigid. I stared at a spot on the ceiling and lay arrow-straight and tight. I couldn't relax. They had gotten a call late in the night to go party at their friend's house, so they scooped me up, carried me to the party, and laid me on a strange bed to sleep while they drank and did lines downstairs.

By the time I was nine, I wanted to die. I felt alone in that house with our heavy secrets. I didn't fit in with the kids in school with my thick glasses, Patch the Pony eyepatch, and pigtails. I was legally blind in my left eye at that age. The only way the doctors could strengthen the bad eye was to have me wear a patch over the good eye to force my bad eye to work harder. Hence, Patch the Pony. My best friend from preschool had moved to Connecticut, and the mean, cool girls hadn't let me in with them, yet. My brother and I fought constantly. At nine, I already knew how to make my dad his glass tumbler full of vodka and ice with a tiny splash of orange juice. I already knew how to cook hotdogs in beer and to make sure to puncture the hot dog with a fork so the beer would soak into it while it boiled, and how to make rice pilaf, and how to lie to my Hebrew school carpool about why my mom couldn't drive that day. I already knew that if she just drank vodka and skipped those white pills that her words wouldn't become slurred. My stomach always burned.

I knew, by age nine, that I had to be a good girl so that I wouldn't cause any more stress in my house. I knew that my dad would come home every night after working eighty hours a week, having missed every game, every play, and every dinner, and that he would drink all night while my mom was sleeping. I knew that his way of loving her was to do anything to protect her, and that meant we were forbidden to tell the truth from as early on as I can remember.

Chapter 9:

No More Apologies

I don't know how old I was, but my brother, who wasn't old enough to drive, was old enough to recognize when someone shouldn't drive. On a cold Cleveland night, we were on our way to take Adam to therapy or a tutor or somewhere else boring, and we stopped at Taco Bell for dinner. By the time we sat down with our food, my mom's mouth was open, her thick tongue was hanging out of her mouth, her eyes were glazed, and her speech was slurred.

We knew she needed to eat something to soak up whatever poison she had taken. She was a mess and things didn't go well from there. This was not the first time we drove in a car while one of our parents was drunk or high. It was just the first time it got so intense and out of control.

My brother refused to get into the car: "I'm not getting in the car with you!" My mom did what parents do when their kids won't get in the car: She started driving away, but she wasn't kidding. She was really going to leave him. I screamed from the back seat and hit her shoulder. "Mom, please stop! Mom, please!"

Adam was shouting outside the car, running alongside it, and knocking on the window. "Stop the car!" We finally got her to stop and let Adam in. He must have only gotten in because he was scared to let me go alone, or to be abandoned and on his own, or to let her drive alone.

We ended up getting lost in a part of town I had never seen. We convinced our mom to pull over to get gas. Trying to get a drunk adult to do anything is exhausting, and this was only accomplished with lots of yelling and crying and begging.

As soon as the car stopped, Adam grabbed the keys and ran to a payphone. My dad was, of course, at work still, so he sent one of his employees to pick us up. The next morning, our dad called us into their bedroom where we saw our mom. The scene was always the same: balled up tissues on the nightstand, a half-empty glass of water sweating under the lamp, her tearstained and swollen face against the pillow. There was mascara smeared under her puffy eyes, and her hair still smelled like perfume and cigarettes from the night before. I stood unmoving at first, filled with disgust and fear that rose like heat from the bottom of my stomach to my face. "Go give your mom a hug," my dad always said. My mom would prop up on her side of the bed, waiting for our forgiveness. Only this time, the morning after we got lost in her car, something had changed in me. I no longer felt sorry for my mom or my dad. I went through the motions anyway. I stepped forward and mechanically hugged her. I spoke whatever words they expected. But I did it red-faced and angry. I did it so that the ordeal would be over faster.

That day, I stopped believing what she mumbled in her tearful apologies. It became like a dance that we did. She'd do these steps, and we'd do those. But I could no longer find any feeling in the music. Because I knew we would be back in her bedroom again and again with her crying and apologizing and promising that things were going to change. We would do what we had to do to make her stop crying, and we would go on, back to the lonely house of lies and secrets.

The burning house of my past raged on inside me, getting hotter. In the hallway, I stacked up boxes and threw full garbage bags on top. No one could see me through the clutter, the heat, and the smoke. I was in this alone.

Chapter 10:

A Fork in the Road

It all ended, when I was thirteen, on an uneventful note at Lulu and Papa Harry's house. We were there for one of the Jewish holidays. My mom had passed out in her chicken soup, nodding off before the prayers were finished. My dad ran around apologizing: "She has really bad PMS and took something for her cramps." My brother and I rolled our eyes. Lulu said, "Alan, her head almost fell in her soup!"

My dad backpedaled. "She's been very stressed." My brother shoved his chair back, which screeched against the marble floor, and he burst up from his seat. He walked out the front door and slammed it shut. All eyes followed, looking toward their usually quiet grandson sitting on the front steps. Lulu followed Adam, and I went out with her. She put her arm around him.

Adam shook his head and said, "I'm not getting in the car with my mom." My mouth dropped open. I couldn't believe it. He had broken the code and told Lulu.

And that was it. Lulu marched back inside with a purpose. We were told to watch TV while the grown-ups talked. I wasn't there for the conversation that would change our entire lives. I was there for the aftermath. Apparently, Lulu had known all along. She had gone to the hospital when my mom was taken there after overdosing. She had seen my mom slur and seen my dad guzzle all of those cases of vodka. Mom and Dad were not fooling anyone, but seeing her first grandson refuse to get in the car was what pushed Lulu into action. She told them that if they didn't get the help they needed that she would take us. She sent them to Jewish Family Services, where my mom passed the alcohol assessment test with flying colors and where my dad went just for support but also ended up passing the test. And then everything changed.

But I would miss out on a lot of it because I had already started drinking and popping diet/speed pills when I was nine. We turned into the proverbial passing ships: Them coming home from a meeting while I sailed out the door to a party. Them with their nightly recovery meetings and me with my increasing self-loathing, anorexia, and boy craziness. I couldn't hear them, and they couldn't stop me.

My dad got sober and continued his nonstop work schedule. He still missed most of my activities, but he was less angry and laughed more. My mom completely changed. She became present and showed up for everything. She never passed out again. She drove for the carpool. She became everything I ever wanted during those years I was so alone, but it was too late. As much as I loved her and as close as we became, I was trapped inside myself behind mountains of clutter stuffed in the hallway of a slowly burning house. The only way to cope with it was by pouring and putting anything in my body that promised to make me forget it all.

Where we come from matters. I was full of the murder and the forest and the bombs and the fire. I was full of the secrets and the pretending. And this is who I was when I stood on the edge of the beginning of my end.

From my story comes a well full of gratitude. The thank-yous in this section are for each teacher and each life lesson that has made the mosaic of all that I am today.

Dear Patch the Pony,

That was the name the cool kids at school called you when the doctor made you wear an eyepatch. It wasn't bad enough that you had to wear glasses that were Coke-bottle thick and made your one eye look tiny next to your other eye, but you also had to wear the patch every day. And every single day, the kids would laugh and say, "Here comes Patch the Pony." And you would hate to go to school. And you cried and told your mom. What I want to thank you for is the frame of reference, and empathy, and understanding you gave me. You humbled me and taught me how it feels when the mean kids target you and how I never want to make anyone feel that way, ever. You also helped me learn how to parent. I have told my three boys about you, and they know the stories. In a span of three weeks, each came home having been made fun of because of their glasses, or having been called "gay," or having been bullied on the bus. I was able to hug them, and allow my heart to break with them, and tell them I understood. And I didn't say anything useless like, "sticks and stones . . ." because words do hurt, and the memory of them never leaves you. And I was able to tell each of them to feel the feeling they were experiencing and ask themselves if they ever wanted to make anyone feel the way they do. And we were able to celebrate the kids who stood up for them, and we reminded each other that being one of the kids who stands up for the one being made fun of is more important than the car you drive, the college you get into, or the amount of money in your bank account. In fact, you taught me that how we treat others matters more than anything at all.

Part Two:
The Forest

Chapter 11:

I Hate Everything About You

The first time I got drunk, it was on Manischewitz
wine during Passover dinner at Lulu and Papa Harry's
two-family home. The house smelled of garlic and
cooking oil. Booze flowed, and the white noise of constant,
overlapping conversations hummed. The adults laughed at me
when I chugged shot glasses full of wine. No one monitored
the amount I took. Before I knew it, I was slap-happy wasted.

I was wearing one of my mom's outfits that she made me
promise not to spill anything on, or she would "kill me." It
was tan suede, and we had to safety pin the waist. At some
point, while drunk, I piled all of the *kippahs* on top of my
head and pulled down my pants in front of everyone. It was a
blast. I didn't get in trouble. My mom might have had a talk
with me about not pulling my pants down in front of people.

After that, my thoughts and feelings and energy were
becoming tangled and messy. I became obsessed with my body
and my weight. I studied my mom as she drank her diet sodas,
and smoked her cigarettes, and removed the bun from her
McDonald's burgers, and marched in front of the TV while
Jane Fonda shouted encouraging words. My mom was always
dieting and exercising and worrying how she looked. But to
me, she was gorgeous and didn't need to do a thing. But if she
thought *she* was fat, then I knew I was, too.

By middle school, I ran every single day, did *Abs and Buns of Steel*, and followed a very restrictive diet. My diet consisted of three pretzel sticks, a grapefruit at lunch (so the other students wouldn't notice me not eating), and sometimes, some cold cereal at night if I had worked out enough. I hated everything about me. I would stare in the mirror for hours, picking apart everything I didn't like. I could never get skinny enough or pretty enough. I never felt enough.

Some kids at school called me Carl after my long hair had to be chopped off when a highlight went horribly wrong. It wasn't the first time I had been made fun of and wouldn't be the last. But it hurt. I remember having to show up to a bar mitzvah with my new Demi Moore circa *Ghost* haircut, minus the boobs. I was flat-chested, and my period still hadn't come. As my mom joked, I could wear my training bra backwards, and it wouldn't make a difference. I was so anxious for puberty to start and make my boobs grow that I brought a pad with me wherever I went, just in case.

If my mom said anything to me about eating, I shut her down and walked away. I had a hate/hate relationship with mirrors. I spent a great deal of time sitting on the 1970's speckled gold and white counter in the green tiled bathroom examining my face and body up close in the mirror. No matter how much I sucked in my belly, it never looked like the hard and flat midsections of the girls on *Baywatch*.

When my body did shrink and grow in all the right places, I started wearing Daisy Dukes and carrying my Walkman. I listened to explicit mixtapes with songs like "She Swallowed It," as I cut through people's yards to my middle school. When I got to school, I would be sent back home to change, and I'd miss first period almost daily. Our principal stood at the front door inspecting the girls' clothing and sent home the ones with inappropriate outfits. He hated me, and it was mutual.

I was a pain to have in class because I was a smartass and talked all the time, but I always knew the answers when teachers called on me. I had undiagnosed ADD and a boyfriend that carried a butterfly knife and wore a beeper (for what, I have no idea). We were in Beachwood, Ohio, which was similar to the 90210 but with Jews.

Chapter 12:

So You Think You Could Tell?

I was thirteen when I went to my first concert (Pink Floyd) in the old Cleveland Stadium. It was a few months before my parents got sober. I walked into the arena, and it smelled like my mom's perfume. When the lights came on and the first chords of "Comfortably Numb" came booming from the speakers, I could feel the release and promise of a space without heat and pain in my chest. I understood why being numb was the solution for my parents, and I knew that I wanted to get lost in that world as soon as possible.

There was no one to talk to about what was really happening. My brother hid in his room, blasting Jimi Hendrix and playing his guitar. We couldn't tell anyone what was going on at home. "Don't tell Lulu," had become my parents' mantra. I couldn't talk to my friends, with their perfect stay-at-home moms who would buy them clothes from the mall for parties and ask them how they were doing.

My parents were a mess. Most days, my mom was passed out on the couch when I got home from school, and my dad was always at work. They were at the very end of their alcoholism, though I had no way of knowing it, and I wanted someone to find me hiding inside myself, blocked off by a cluttered fire hazard of a hallway, crouching and terrified in a hot, airless, little room.

My best friend, Stephanie, and I would ride our ten-speeds to Heights Pharmacy. She would talk to the cashier and buy candy while I stole diet pills and No-Doz and hid them in my Bubble Tape case. The first few I took were magical because they made me perky and energetic. I found a magic pill that finally worked. I became silly and non-stop Carly.

I took the No-Doz for a while to help me study. When that wasn't enough, I took speed. I was still a straight-A student because of speed and, also, because I had learned in our house that if you kept your outsides looking good, you'd fool everyone. Daily speed and the few times we could steal our parents' liquor became the little islands I swam to for relief. But the first time I got truly shitfaced drunk was the night before the Thanksgiving of my thirteenth year.

I was sleeping at Stephanie's house. She was my ticket into the cool girl group, and I could feel myself in its margins. The position felt too precarious. But I knew how to deal with social anxiety. The rest of the cool girls in our cool girl group of seventh graders were all sleeping over, too. We called ourselves the Six-Pack. These were some of the very same girls who made fun of me, and stomped on my shoes, and called me Patch the Pony, but now I'd made my way in with them. In Stephanie's basement, we devised a scheme to get completely wasted. Stephanie had stolen a bottle of Smirnoff vodka, and one of the other girls brought a handful of beers she took from her parents' stash in their garage.

I held my nose and downed the first can of warm beer right out in the open in Stephanie's driveway. We went to her basement next. I drank more warm beer. I hated beer; it was too bubbly and filling and it took too long to work. But it worked. It impressed the other girls who were watching

Stephanie and I enter this next level of adulthood right there in her basement. I had never felt so funny and attractive. After the beer, the two of us, two skinny thirteen-year-olds, split an entire bottle of vodka on our own. We mixed it with some fruity, sugary drinks, and were out of our minds by 9:00 p.m. Because it was so early, we didn't want to go upstairs to go to the bathroom and risk facing her parents. Instead, we peed in a bucket and hid it in her crawl space. I can only barely, in nonlinear clips, recall what happened next. I came to with my face pressed against the cold tile floor of her bathroom, where I found myself curled by the toilet.

When I got home, I half lied about why I didn't want to eat Thanksgiving dinner. I said I was coming down with a bad sickness, which seemed as true as anything. Shortly after that, my parents got sober. They found recovery meetings, which they went to every night, religiously, while I discovered my incredible stamina for parties with Stephanie, which I did whenever I could.

And as my parents got sober, I began my affair with everything that almost killed them. It was as though we walked through a revolving door together, only in opposite directions. On opposite sides, we watched each other through thick glass, but there was no way for them to reach me or for me to hear them. My mother became what I always needed her to be, but I was too far gone already. Her love was endless and buoyed me, but the need for her approval, which was completely self-propelled, made our relationship the most important and the most emotionally volatile for me. Alcohol was what allowed all the fears and anxiety and pain to lessen.

In the beginning, it felt like I swallowed liquid neon, and I saw myself standing on top of an old muscle car with go-go boots and boas and glitter. I had discovered my secret power. This was the first time in my whole life that I could actually breathe.

The other addiction I picked up soon after was just as destructive and almost as powerful as the booze and drugs. I always needed to have a boy to obsess over because if someone wanted me, then I was good enough. Guys were tied to my insatiable need for more. I had to have someone who wanted me, and I had to have multiple guys on the back burner, just in case the relationship didn't work out with the current boyfriend. The idea of being on my own was terrifying. I needed them to tell me I was enough. I could be heartbroken and depressed, and then a guy I liked would call, and I'd become elated and unstoppable.

Chapter 13:
Southern Discomfort

By high school, I had a raging eating disorder. When my mom tried to talk to me about all of the exercise I was doing or food I was not eating, I made it very unpleasant to interact with me. I would cut her off or shut her down with a glare. I was on the track and cross-country teams. I made myself run an extra two miles before school at 10 mph on the treadmill. Sometimes, I would skip lunch to get in a few more extra miles. And then I would run during practice after school with the rest of the team.

Eventually, a stress fracture in my shin turned into a break and because I could not stop myself from working out, I broke my foot from power walking. When I could no longer run on a broken leg or power walk on a broken foot, I made myself "run" in the pool. I was nonstop. I was on student council, yearbook, the school newspaper, and in honors classes.

When my parents got enough sobriety under their belts and tried to assert themselves, giving me boundaries and curfews and consequences, I yelled at them, "A curfew? Now? Why?"

"Because we don't want you out at all hours."

"Oh, now you're going to parent me? I don't know if you're aware of this, but I've been taking care of myself since I was

SECONDS AND INCHES - A MEMOIR

nine!" Anything they came at me with, I came back harder. I was exhausting to argue with. I was inconsiderate and had a smartass answer for everything I did. When they told me I wasn't doing something that I needed to do, I'd argue back, "I get straight A's. I'm in D.A.R.E., and M.A.D.D., and student council, and yearbook, and track. What more do you want from me?" There was no argument for that. No one could catch me.

I kept moving so no one could stop me and tell me I was heading the wrong way. I had no idea that what I was doing to my body would set me up for a lifetime of gastrointestinal issues or that the fight to accept my body as it was would be one that I'd fight for decades to come. The guys I hooked up with used me as much as I used them. When I only drank alcohol, I'd get so wasted that I would throw up and pass out by nine o'clock. My friends and I would be invited to all of the upper-class parties because we were the pretty girls. There, I found that I could keep up with the older guys in whatever drinking game was being played. I liked taking shots and drinking Zimas because they were faster and had fewer calories. I needed to quiet the feelings and also, always, keep my outside looking good. The perfect mask to hide behind.

What I wouldn't give to spend just one hour with the broken girl I was in high school. What I wouldn't give to tell her that none of this was important and that I needed to get to a place where I could value myself and honor who I was. But I wasn't ready for that kind of honesty, and it would take a lot more destruction and pain before that broken girl would rebuild herself into a woman of dignity.

One guy I dated was a football-obsessed lineman. We constantly watched football tapes, and he told me he didn't like girls who drank, so I disguised myself for him and completely gave up alcohol. About three weekends in, I was dejected and bored. I hated how I felt, sitting at parties, drinking Gatorade, and pretending I was having fun. I remember sitting in his car and listening to "Better Man" by Pearl Jam and feeling so unhappy. Being sober with myself out in the world left me feeling raw and exposed.

The following weekend, I was at a frat house with two girlfriends while visiting the University of Michigan, where we went regularly to party with the college crowd. The frat boys were having an Around-the-World theme party, and I went to the Texas room to get myself a full cup of Southern Comfort. It had been about three weeks since I'd had a drink, and I couldn't stand what sober felt like. I didn't even like the football player boyfriend anymore. I just wanted to be wanted. But my desire for alcohol outweighed my desire to be wanted by him, so alcohol won. I took my Southern Comfort and sat on the first two steps of the staircase. I drank a big gulp and felt the warm liquor fill my insides. In that moment, I made the decision that I would never let a guy, or anyone, come in between me and drinking ever again. The football boyfriend broke up with me the following week when he heard about my binge. *Fuck it*, I thought.

Dear AP Physics Teacher,

I learned one of the most valuable lessons in all of high school in your class. I still remember what it felt like when you humiliated me, and it helps me be the teacher, mother, friend, and human I am today. I didn't end up in AP Physics by mistake. I was doing well in AP Calculus, and the guidance counselor thought it made sense for me to try your class. Science was never my strongest subject. When I'd raise my hand in your class, you wouldn't hide your annoyance. You'd say, "Oh look, Carly has another question!" You joked, "Let me guess, Carly doesn't understand what I just explained." I was your favorite play toy in class. And everyone laughed except for me. I endured you the entire year. I barely got by with a C. I was stressed and confused and hated going to your class each day. And when it was all over, and you were packing up your class for the summer, and I was getting ready to graduate, I came into your classroom and told you that I would never enjoy science because of you. I said it calmly, and you tried to backpedal, but it was too late. The damage had been done, and the lesson had solidified. When I became a teacher and a mother myself, I knew that I would never make a student or subordinate who knew less than me feel how you made me feel. Thank you for that gift. Not all of the gifts we get from the universe come with a bow, but I believe your gift will help so many more people than you could have ever reached yourself.

Chapter 14:

My Drug of Choice Was, "Yes, Please"

Junior year in high school, I fell in love with Miles Baker. He was artsy, dark, super smart, and protective of me. He was the kind of boyfriend that would fight with me and for me and that kind of intensity was what I craved. We were inseparable. He and the guys he hung out with smoked pot and did drugs and got tattoos, and I felt like I had found my people. The night I got high for the first time, I felt like I'd been granted entry to a secret, exclusive world that I didn't know existed before. At first, I felt nothing. And then, I felt everything. I remember thinking, *I am going to get high as often as I possibly can.* Getting high was perfection because when I just drank, I threw up and passed out. But getting high removed all the anxiety about what others thought, the tension in my belly, and the concern about saying the right words and wearing the right outfit. It brought me to a beautiful place of giving absolutely no fucks.

Once that door opened, I wanted to know and experience everything the world of drugs had to offer. Before that high even wore off, I was planning how I could get more. I would have tried and done whatever was handed to me. It is only by seconds and inches that I have survived to tell my story.

There was always alcohol, and the drugs helped me drink more without getting sick after. I found acid and started tripping every day, and my mind expanded to see realities I didn't know existed. When I was high, I felt like I was finally standing in my truth, but I could never recall that truth when I was sober. I laughed and touched myself and hugged my friends and saw lights and was able to walk and run endlessly and feel the superhero-like strength in my body.

One early morning, I drove home after a heavy night of drugs. I was still high and my contacts had dried out in my eyes, so I drove very slowly with my face all but pressed to the windshield. I could barely see. It took me fifteen minutes to drive one mile with no traffic. Somehow, I parked my car and crawled into bed safely before my 4:00 a.m. curfew. I'd humored my parents by allowing them to give me a curfew but negotiated it back to where it basically didn't matter anymore. There were many other nights like that. When I think back to those nights driving high, I get hot in the face to think of all the accidents I could've caused and people I could've easily hurt or killed.

When Miles, who was a year ahead of me in school, left for college, I was devastated. My shoulders slumped when I dragged myself to the mall to spray his Polo Ralph Lauren cologne on the necklace he gave me, so I could smell him still. I was convinced he was cheating on me with those free and confident college girls in his dorm. I drove with a friend in my car, Rhonda the Red-Hot Honda, blasting Kenny Wayne Shepherd and Guns N' Roses as we headed to West Virginia University for the weekend to visit him. When we arrived, Miles rolled a huge blunt laced with coke. After smoking it, I felt like I was trapped in one of those old, broken box TV sets that buzz with static and little black and white dots on the screen.

My senior year, I checked out. I lost interest in being popular. It was exhausting to have to look a certain way, act a certain way, and pretend I liked people I didn't really like. I learned I had almost enough credits to graduate early and took an internship at a radio station downtown while attending the one class I still needed to complete. I had relatively decent grades and could have gotten into many schools, but I went to Ohio University. The biggest qualifier for this school was that, when I visited, my fake ID worked at the local bars. I also heard that OU was really close to Meigs County, which was the pot-growing capital of Ohio. I needed to be with like-minded people who liked to get high as much as I did. Miles and I were still together, and after I left, we missed each other so much that he transferred to OU to be with me.

Chapter 15:

College Bound

The night before I left for college, all the girls and I went to Shooters, a massive bar on the water that was stuck in the '80s and was easy on girls with fake IDs. I had fifteen shots of tequila, got in a fight with my friends about an earring I lost, and threw up all night long. I thought I was going to die like Hendrix. But instead, the next day I had to drive with my parents in their new SUV to Athens, Ohio, where I barely knew a soul, to start my college life.

I made the choice to go to a school where I knew no one, in part, because I wanted to stop being the person I had become. There was no way to know then that the dorm I was in combined with the major I chose wouldn't help to cause the kind of change I craved. I remained sick the entire way to school and had to make my parents stop at just about every other rest area bathroom. "I'm just really nervous," I said as an excuse. Tequila became the only alcohol I would never touch again.

After we set up my room and bed, we hugged, and I walked them to the parking lot, where my mom and I both fell apart. Her, maybe at the thought of no longer being together, or perhaps because she was afraid of what I would do when I really let loose. Me, because I was desperate, and scared, and temporarily without alcohol in my body.

After the tearful embrace, my mom handed me a thick envelope. "Don't open this until you get back to your room. You're going to be great. And don't forget to call. I have the new 1-800 number all set up for you." The card was full of extra spending cash, an angel pin, and one of her long, heartfelt letters telling me how proud she was, how I was going to make new friends, and how she was always there for me. It made me realize how alone I actually was. How I was going to get my wish, and be on my own, and know almost no one.

I remembered the bag of pot I'd brought, hidden in my locked CD trunk. I grabbed the baggie, walked across the hall, and knocked on the door. Ryan and her roommate were setting up their room, and I quietly said, "Hey, I'm your new neighbor"—holding up the bag—"wanna smoke?" And just like that, I was set. I had my new friends, and I was stoned out of my mind. Miles wasn't arriving for a few days, and my new friends and I got dressed up, blasted Barenaked Ladies, and headed out to find a party.

Chapter 16:

Fuck Everything and Run

At college, I felt like I could reinvent myself. No one knew about what I did in high school. At OU, I would be free and chill and fun—anything went. The thought of being tied down to my high school boyfriend, hanging out at his place, sharing the living room with his dad—it made me feel like I was slowly dying. I wanted to get out and be free. After the first few days of long nights, parties, guys catcalling all the new freshman, late night burrito runs (I only ate when I was wasted), and climbing the huge hill up to Court Street, I decided that he would just get in my way.

At my very first class, Intro to Theater History, I realized that I wanted to be a theater major. I sat in the auditorium listening to a professor who spoke about it in a way that made me want to jump into his brain and stay forever. All the girls in the theater were wacky and unbridled and dressed like artsy hippies. The guys were outgoing and verbose and hysterical. These were my people.

And then I saw him: Theo. He turned around, we locked eyes, and there was a physical, electric connection. I could no longer hear or see anyone else. All I could see was his dark hair and eyes that pierced directly through my clothes. He came up to me as we were pouring out of the theater and gave me some line about, "Don't I know you?" I left with his number, and he left with the name of my dorm.

The next two years were a blur of drunken nights, tripping on shrooms, tripping on acid, and rolling on Ecstasy as I wandered from dorm room to house party. The free, neon, glowing girl I felt like when I first began drinking is who I became, but a darker version. A version who hated herself and was always looking for a new way to stop the feelings.

I wore go-go boots and glitter and dresses over pants and boas of every color. Some nights, I wore hippie tops with no bra. Others, I wore my hair wet and slicked back, dressed in all black, covered myself in glitter, and walked around with my pupils so big I honestly thought my green eyes had turned black. I made out with other people's boyfriends and left a trail of glitter on their faces. I had no moral compass. I never stopped to consider how my behavior affected anyone else. I remember my mother shouting at me, "You think the whole world revolves around you!" and having no idea what she was talking about. The best word to describe me back then would be inconsiderate. Unless it directly affected me, I simply didn't consider anyone else.

One night, I was hanging out at Theo's place, waiting for him to get off work, when Halle, the girl he was in *Romeo & Juliet* with, came knocking on the door looking for me. She was an upperclassman. Gorgeous and confident, she smelled of musk perfume and had lavish, curly, brown hair. "I feel bad telling you this, and I totally would not have let anything happen had I known you and Theo were together . . ." she paused, her face an apology. "Carly, we have been sleeping together for the past month, since we started the show. I'm so sorry. I had no idea about you until today."

I couldn't hear a word she said after that. I felt nauseated and dizzy. I could hardly breathe. I tried not to believe her, but then she said he was at her apartment right then, and she would take me to him. In her car on the way, she continued to apologize. I wondered how she found out about me and what made her care so much, but I didn't ask any questions or say anything.

We walked in, and it was a party scene. A bunch of people I didn't know surrounded Theo, who had just taken a hit from a joint. He squinted at me, holding his breath, and croaked, "Carly? What are you doing here?"

"Halle came over and told me."

He played innocent. "Told you what?"

"Told me about you two."

He stood up and grabbed my arm to pull me outside. I remember standing under a streetlamp, shouting at him with mascara-stained cheeks. I knew that this must be love because why else would it hurt so bad? And he must have loved me, too, because he cried.

"I don't know what the fuck is wrong with me. I don't know why it's so hard to do this with you."

"Do what? What are we even doing?"

"Carly, you're the only girl who has ever made me want to be honest. It's like you force it out of me. And I want to be honest with you."

We walked back to his place, crying and fighting, then we fell into his bed. And just like that, I took him back. That night, I gave up enough of myself that by the next afternoon, I could not exist in my own skin. I had to get high just to get through the afternoon. And when I got high on purpose, to make the pain quieter, it worked. I felt better.

Chapter 17:

Not Enough

A few weeks later, Theo said to me, "I need to not be in a relationship." He air quoted "relationship." He had come up with a new plan, one so insane that I agreed. The plan was that we would be in an open relationship. We could be with whoever we wanted, but we would also be together. We would still move in together, but not as boyfriend and girlfriend, just as roommates. And if we were going to spend the night with someone else, we were not to call home and let the other know because that would be too cruel. He wanted his freedom, and he wanted me. I just wanted him, and I also wanted to hurt him for not thinking I was enough.

The next morning, I felt scared and unsafe, like at any moment I would be caught. I almost expected the police to break through the door, shouting and pulling out handcuffs. I balled up on the couch and cried. Theo saw me and packed a bowl. He sat beside me. "Smoke this. You'll feel better."

And I did feel better. I wrote better. I walked better. I no longer felt the pain. I felt like he couldn't touch me. It was the first time I deliberately got high with the goal to dull the pain. I was no longer getting high for fun. I wasn't getting high to hang with friends. I was getting high to escape where I was. It was the day when the boomerang of alcoholism and drug addiction switched directions. I would learn about this later in sobriety: how the alcoholic crosses an invisible line, where the booze and drugs stop being fun and start being necessary.

The amount I needed to put into my body to get high enough or drunk enough became infinite. I needed to quiet the voices within me that were telling me to leave, then telling me to stay, then telling me he was going to hurt me again. I became darker and angrier. I made it my mission to hook up with as many of Theo's friends as I could. If he wanted an open relationship, he would have one.

Chapter 18:

Costumes and Masks

Our apartment was centrally located on Court Street, on the corner above Perk's coffee shop. It smelled of burnt beans roasting mixed with the smell of the freshly baked pizza from the ovens next door at Goodfella's. It was close to the theater building and all the bars.

I painted every wall midnight blue with bright yellow stars as Theo warned me he wouldn't help me cover it up when the landlord saw what I did. I painted all the trim fire island orange. I splatter painted the kitchen and covered the futon with furry cow print fabric. We placed our double beds in the one bedroom we had since we were just roommates. They were separated by about four inches. There was constant Nag Champa incense burning. Our apartment was the trippy stop along the way to the bars.

Because of the house I grew up in, I knew that no one could really bother me about not doing well if I was getting good grades. I studied hard, and I took tons of notes. I thrived in theater. I loved learning, and I, especially, loved my playwriting classes. I'd write my papers, and then I'd write papers for Theo but from a different point of view and with a different tone, so the professors wouldn't catch on that it wasn't his work. When my mom asked how school was going, I would be able to tell her, "Great! All A's."

As soon as my homework was done, I would start to party. The only time I would stop ingesting drugs or alcohol was right before auditions. Theater was the one world I held more sacred than anything else. If auditions for the quarter were on Friday night, I would stop using Tuesday and be clean for auditions. I loved performing. In fact, I loved all aspects of the theater. When I was on stage performing a monologue, it felt like I was glowing and closer to who I really was than I'd ever been.

As soon as auditions were over, I would race back to our apartment and get as high as possible because I couldn't go to see the posted callback sheet sober. I was too afraid to feel whatever I would feel if my name wasn't on that sheet. I couldn't stand in front of the other theater people and look at that list without being high.

Instead, I would go home, get stoned, and wait until the middle of the night, after everyone had already checked for their names and went back home to get into bed so they would be fresh for the early morning callback. Only then would I stumble down the alley to Kantner Hall to see if I made it on the list.

I would see my name and race home to get ready for my callback. It was exhausting. I was exhausted. My grades were better than they'd ever been. I made the Dean's List every quarter. But I was vibrating with anxiety. I dropped every course that wasn't theater, dance, or English. On the outside, I had it all, but on the inside, I could barely hold all of the plates I was trying to spin in the air. I fantasized about how I could end it all.

All I could do was imagine a time when I was no longer alive. I felt untethered and, at the same time, trapped. I spent a great deal of time thinking about my own death. How I wanted out, how I no longer wanted to feel all these feelings. I was sick of feeling so out of control. I began seeing a therapist from the Student Health Center. He was an older man who made me sign a contract stating I wouldn't kill myself. I laughed when he gave it to me and asked him, "What will you do if I break my promise?" He didn't think I was funny.

He said, "There is something wrong inside of you. You're like one of those cars the manufacturing company recalls because it is unsafe to be on the road, but the mechanics can't figure out what's wrong."

I stole from grocery stores because all the money my parents sent for food went to drugs and booze. I began chain-smoking cigarettes and doing so much Ecstasy that my dentist told me I had shaved a layer of enamel off my molars from grinding. With each high, I found moments of peace, where I didn't have a care in the world. But with each comedown, I found myself sinking deeper into panic and despair.

With our open relationship and my attempts to punish Theo, I met a really cool human named Liam. Liam was a smart and snarky scientist. He kept dead bugs in clear, glass containers in his room and wore Lucky Jeans that had "Lucky You" on the inside of his fly. His roommate Jack (who was dating a theater friend of mine) introduced us one night over a card game. He was good-looking in that 1950's kind of way, and he found me to be amusing and intriguing.

The first night we hooked up, he told me a riddle. He asked me, "Where are you?" and I guessed every answer but never got it right.

"Athens, your porch, in your arms, America, the world, Ohio," but he just pulled on his cigarette and laughed at me.

Finally, he told me, "You are here."

I punched him in the arm. He laughed and said he had another one: "What time is it?"

Back and forth we went again, but all of my answers were wrong.

Eventually, he said, "Now. The time is now." And just like that, I was in love again.

Liam didn't know about Theo, but Theo knew about Liam, and he didn't like it. He got extremely jealous when he found out. It was the sick game we played. Theo and I would hook up at night, and be roommates during the day. He wouldn't be my boyfriend. He wouldn't give me that part of himself. As soon as I'd meet someone I actually liked, it was as if Theo abruptly turned off the music and put on a different song. He'd become attentive, and clingy, and would ask lots of questions about where I was going and who I would be with. He'd treat me the way I always wished he would, but by the time I met Liam, I was bored with the games.

Liam and I went on nature walks, explored each other's bodies, laughed, smoked American Spirits and pot, snuggled and showered together, but I would always make him drive me home late at night, with the excuse of needing to get up early. I couldn't let Theo stay at the apartment all night without me. I wanted to torture him with the smell of Liam all over me. And it worked. Each night after I came home, into my bed Theo would climb. And as he smelled Liam all over me, I smelled jealousy all over him, and I hated myself a little more because I couldn't resist him. Every time I got strong enough to move on, he turned the music back on and pulled me into that dance with him. I wanted to just be done, but I was drawn in every time.

I also began seeing a psychiatrist connected to O'Bleness Hospital who prescribed me a different medication every three weeks. In that doctor's office, I found myself in the vicious cycle of telling him what was wrong with me, acquiring a new prescription to try, then mixing the prescription with my own drugs, and then showing back up in search of something stronger. I didn't know how I'd be able to go on like this, but I couldn't stop that cycle either.

On one of the medications, I stayed up until four in the morning scrubbing my carpet. Sometimes, it felt like I couldn't get the walls to stop closing in on me or the voices in my head to shut up. I remember telling one of my professors that it felt like my insides were curling up and dying. I broke up with Liam, and ignored Theo, and started isolating.

Chapter 19:

Liar, Liar

I called my mom and told her how horrible the college therapist was. "Mom, he wants me to sign a suicide contract."

"A what?"

"He wants me to sign a contract promising I won't kill myself." I heard her catch her breath.

"What is he going to do if I don't follow through with the contract?"

"Carly, how much are you using?"

"I don't know."

"Well, are you using a lot?"

"What's a lot?"

"Are you using a lot? Like two times per week?"

I am not a liar. I am a truth teller. I was not using a couple of times a week. I was using every single day. From morning until night. Therefore, I was not using "a lot," which is a couple times per week. "Not a lot," I said.

At the time, I believed I had answered her question honestly, but looking back, I was not capable of being honest. I wasn't being honest with myself. I had to construct my own house of cards in order to be okay with all of my choices. I always had a justification in my mind, just in case someone asked.

She never hesitated; she never kept quiet with the sobriety talk. "What about trying to not use anything at all? Could you do that?"

I'd never tried to not use at all. Not since high school, and that sucked.

"I'm just worried that the using is making your moods worse. You know, making you more depressed."

"Mom, I'm depressed because I'm not on the right medication. They can't find the right medication."

"But what if you just tried to see if it helps to be off everything else?"

I was sure her support group had told her there was nothing she could do for me, but she didn't stop trying anyway. Instead, she sent me pamphlets and care packages and letters and called me and wrote to me and checked on me every single day. I would tell her how much I was struggling, and I would write plays in playwriting class about a young woman who couldn't look in the mirror and was dying to get help but couldn't take care of herself. I did not see the connection.

"Are you asking God for help?" My mom had taught me to talk to God when she first got sober. She taught me the Serenity Prayer and to ask God for help when I needed it. Before she got sober, we never talked about God in our house.

"I can't hear God anymore. He can't hear me."

I began snorting Special K, which is also used as a horse tranquilizer. Theo and our theater friend christened me with my first K-bump one evening at his apartment. I heard Radiohead screaming in the background, and the cinder block walls of his basement started coming closer. The two of them pushed me into his tiny shower stall, saying that's what you're supposed to do your first time on K. So I stood there, fully clothed, dripping wet, clueless as to how I got into the shower or where my hands came from.

On K, the dreamlike atmosphere inside my head accelerated. K removed the safety lever in my head and allowed every choice I made to be unfiltered—no more considerations of logic. I put every and any drug I got my hands on in my mouth. The world around me felt like a ride I couldn't get off of. At night before I passed out, I would beg God to not let me wake up. And when I did, I felt betrayed.

Chapter 20:

Restless, Irritable & Discontent

In the late fall of my sophomore year, my mom must have been tired enough of hearing me complain to offer me a challenge: "Can you go just three weeks without getting drunk or high?" Other than that pitifully short time in high school when I was dating the football player who didn't like girls who drank, I had never tried to stop. "I don't think you can," she said. And that was it. I'd show her.

Within the first few days of stopping, I could no longer sleep. If I did nod off, I was tortured with constant graphic nightmares. During the days, it was as though my skin had been removed and someone had pushed me out into the sun. I wanted to physically harm people who pissed me off, which was everyone. But that was rarely an issue because no one wanted to be around me.

I clawed my way through those three weeks by staying mostly alone in my room, smoking, and watching TV. But I made it through three weeks with no drugs or alcohol, which convinced me that alcohol and drugs were not the problem. Because I felt so out of control without anything in my body, I knew there was something really wrong with my mental state.

I decided I just needed to find the right medication to make me feel normal. And that until I found the right medication and the right doctor, I should have a little drink or a little hit off that bowl to calm down. What I felt when I got high for the first time after those three awful weeks was what it feels like when you're swimming at night and you have to get out of the pool to go pee, and you're wet and freezing, and then you run back to the pool and jump in and feel the warmth all around you. That was how it felt when I came back to what I loved. It felt like someone had turned up Led Zeppelin, and the sun was shining on my face, and my feet were on the dashboard, and everything was perfect. After that first night back, I said that there was no reason to ever stop using again. And off I went.

I'd been isolating, so I was cut off from the usual people I partied with. One night, I had a party at our apartment in an attempt to reconnect with the crowd. But during the party, something I took made me believe all the people were intruders trying to attack me, so I made everyone get out and locked the door. I curled up on the floor in the middle of the room, and trembled, and smoked. Someone banged on the door and shouted, "Carly! Let us in! Carly!"

I covered my ears and curled tighter. I couldn't get comfortable. No matter how I moved, it was as if I was lying on nails. There was nowhere I could place myself where I could rest.

Chapter 21:

Shoeless in an Ice Storm

B y winter break of my sophomore year, I was trying again to be sober and failing. But I was crazy when I was drunk or high and crazy when I was sober. Nothing worked. I thought going away would help, so Theo and I decided to go on another road trip to Florida, which we'd done the previous winter break. I made him promise not to drink or use if we went because I was trying to stay sober. But as soon as we hit the road, out came his pipe and up to my mouth it went. Then I had to move the line I had drawn in the sand and draw a new one. I announced, "I'm only going to get high on this trip."

We came back to Athens for New Years, and I was ready to follow through on my promise of Ohio sobriety. But I was suffering, and spiritless, and despised everyone around me. So I decided I'd stop on January 1st. Only I don't remember anything else until January 20th.

On the weekend of the twentieth, there was an ice storm in Athens, and all the bars and stores were closed. I couldn't get any alcohol or get out of the house to get drugs, and I lost it. I felt something crack in my sanity, and I wanted off the planet. I called O'Bleness Hospital to check myself in because I didn't feel safe on my own anymore. I knew I was falling apart, and I knew I would do something dangerous if I didn't get help, but no one answered the phone. I left the apartment in the middle of the night, without boots or a coat, and wandered the streets looking for something.

Chapter 22:

If You Want It, Come and Get It

While walking the streets at night in an ice storm, somehow freezing and hot at the same time, I thought about Grace. I'd done a four show black box production with a dynamic group of artists. Grace was one of the directors. One night during the production when we were downing drinks at an afterparty, I noticed that she wasn't. I asked her why she wasn't drinking, and she told me she was sober. I filed that away. She had so much confidence, and strength, and she owned whatever space she was in. I spent my time rehearsing lines on the floor on my back because I was usually too hungover from the night before to stand.

I needed to call Grace. I needed help, and there was no one else I could ask. I needed her to tell me what to do. When I got to my apartment, frozen and panicked, I called her. Her phone rang and rang. I knew if she didn't pick up I wouldn't have the courage to call her in the morning. As soon as she picked up, the tears came. There weren't words for what I was feeling, so I just sobbed and wailed. She told me to breathe and gave me an address to meet her at the next morning. We met at a coffee shop near the theater building. I showed up early, smoked cigarette after cigarette, and downed coffee as I waited for her at a corner booth. When she walked in and sat down across from me, I blurted out, "I'm a mess. I don't know what's going on, but I need help."

She paused in removing her coat and frowned. Her eyes were clear sky and hope. She finished removing her coat, and put her hand on mine, and said, "I'm here." I told her how much I'd been using, and how I tried to stop, and how it made it worse, and I asked, "Do you think I'm an addict or an alcoholic?"

"Sweetie, I can't tell you that. That's a question you're going to have to figure out on your own." I crumpled onto the table and put my face in my hands.

"There's a meeting I go to across the street at 6:00. You can come with me if you want. I'm heading there now."

She wasn't going to make this easy. A meeting? I couldn't believe I needed a meeting. But I nodded and put my hoodie over my head to hide in case anyone there knew me. I followed her across the street at a bit of a distance. I was going to my first meeting. My first meeting. I had been to many meetings before, but they were my parents' meetings. This would be my first meeting for me. But the way Grace invited me seemed like it was of no consequence to her if I came with her or not, and the way she confidently held herself, and the way she didn't seem to need anyone to make her OK, it was all so attractive to me. I just had no idea how I could get from where I was to the other planet she lived on.

The meeting was bright and fluorescent in the church conference room. There was nowhere to hide. The styrofoam coffee cups and the smiling faces of mostly middle-aged townies told me what I needed to know: I didn't belong. Everyone knew Grace. She seemed like a celebrity. Someone handed me a blue book that a bunch of people I didn't know wrote their names and phone numbers in. Someone even wrote, *Perfect child of God.* Someone gave me what looked like a list of rules to read aloud, and I read it. People spoke in turns, but I didn't hear a single word. By the time the meeting was over, everyone was talking and laughing, and I was headed for the exit. Grace had asked me if I had plans after, and I lied and told her I did. I wanted to get the hell away from there. I went home and threw the book on the coffee table and called my mom. "Mom, I went to a meeting!"

Chapter 23:

I Can't Do This

I went to a meeting every night for the next five nights. I'd arrive right as the meeting was starting, so I could avoid talking to anyone, sit in the back of the room, eat Chinese takeout during the meeting, and run for the door the second they were done with their circle prayer, waving and smiling as they called my name. I would go home, and get dressed, and wait to go out. I would go to a party or a bar and tell everyone I was sober. No one believed me or took me seriously.

I told all of my professors and the few friends I had left that I was sober. I told Theo we couldn't use drugs or alcohol in the apartment anymore, but he didn't listen. The novelty of being sober and clearheaded wore off fast. I was so uncomfortable, and I hated the meetings where they said the same irrelevant refrigerator magnet clichés every night. I could barely sleep because of the nightmares, and I felt so isolated. Theo was rarely home anymore; he started seeing someone from one of his classes.

I hadn't put a drug or a drop of alcohol in my body for six days, and it felt like the underside of my skin was sandpaper, and my chest was about to ignite into flames, and no one understood how intolerable it was. My mom was the only person who seemed supportive and happy if I was sober, but if this was sober, I couldn't do it. But when I got high again, it didn't work. I no longer felt free. Instead, I felt like I was being chased by demons, and there was no way to escape them, no matter how much I drank or used.

Theo told me he was going on a date. He told me that he really liked her. I had bought tickets to a show at the Swindle Fish before I had gotten sober six days earlier, and I didn't want to waste the $12, so I invited the roommate of the girl Theo was going on a date with to join me. That night at her apartment, my show companion and a friend of hers were getting high before the show and offered me a hit, but I turned them down at first. I'd made it through the past six nights as a newly sober person and didn't want to ruin my streak. I didn't feel satisfied or proud of myself for saying no, though. I felt trapped and like a fraud.

We walked the three blocks to the bar. Court Street, the main street where we both lived, was mostly populated with bars from one end to the other, with a few music stores and banks in between. I couldn't stop staring at the empty booze bottles by the curb of each bar. The people at the meeting had told me not to drink, even though I thought my only problem was with drugs. But that night, my mouth watered for any tiny amount of booze and backwash at the bottom of those empty bottles.

I contemplated it as I walked between the roommate of Theo's date and her friend—I would be willing to take their heads and crack them together if it meant I could grab those bottles and suck every last drop from the bottoms. Six days without anything in my body, and all I wanted was a strong drink. We arrived at the bar, and I saw the bartender that I had convinced to hook up with me, even though he told me he had a girlfriend at another college. He didn't seem like he wanted to see me, and I felt his disgust as he nodded at me and looked away.

I made my way through the crowd of laughing, hippie/punk college students to the bathroom. I was wearing my favorite sky blue tank top, and when I looked at my body in the mirror, I realized I was finally as emaciated as I wanted to be. Finally, my body was acceptable. But when I caught the reflection of my eyes, I saw a girl who would not make it to twenty.

Chapter 24:

The Darkest Night

Back home, I changed out of the tight bar clothes and put on a flannel shirt and baggie shorts. I slid my Sarah McLachlan CD in and hit repeat, turning it up as loud as it would go. The pain inside was unbearable. I could hardly breathe. I opened that blue book they gave me at the first meeting and saw those names and numbers. Some even had written, *Call me anytime.* But it was 1:30 a.m., and they probably wouldn't even remember who I was. I had only gone to a few meetings.

Instead, I called my brother in Cleveland to ask him for help, but he didn't seem to understand what I was saying. After a few minutes, I told him I felt better and had to go. Even though I had begged Theo to hide our drugs and pipes, I saw a packed bowl on the table, and there was a bottle of vodka in the freezer.

I smoked one cigarette after the next, lighting one with the last. I cried and clenched my fists. I turned Sarah up even louder. I wanted out. My mind was wild.

I heard Theo come home from his date. Without a thought, without saying a word, I pushed past him and slammed the bathroom door shut. There was no sound in the bathroom. He had shut off the CD player, and all I could hear was the echo of our toiletries as I threw brushes and gel aside. I do not remember having a plan. I just remember feeling like a caged animal.

I found the ephedrine pills—the kind of speed they sell truck drivers—and poured the entire bottle into my mouth and swallowed them with water from the running faucet. I turned toward the medicine cabinet. I grabbed bottle after bottle of pills and poured them into my mouth, too. I looked at the pills, threw them back in my mouth, and leaned over the sink to get more water. I took bottles of prescription pills without reading the labels, a bottle of Aleve, and a bottle of Tylenol. I looked at myself in the mirror as I emptied that last bottle into my mouth.

I felt like a burglar who'd torn apart the bathroom. I gripped the edge of the sink and lowered myself down onto the bathroom rug. I closed my eyes. Everything got really quiet.

Down on the red shag rug of the bathroom floor, I waited to die. I couldn't breathe. I curled myself into a ball, and hugged my legs, and started to sob. I knew what I had done. I accepted it. It was what I wanted. I knew the amount I took, and I knew the combination would do what I needed it to do. I wanted to be done. I didn't want to do this anymore. I made my choice. I was done.

As I lay on the bathroom floor slowly dying, I heard a voice. It said my name. It was a man's voice, and it said, "Get up, or you're going to die." After a few more moments, I heard it again. "Carly, call Theo's name and ask for help. You have to ask for help." The voice was insistent. I was so ashamed, but I heard this forceful voice, and it was so definite.

I quietly called for Theo through the bathroom door, but he couldn't hear me. I called again and again until my voice was loud enough for him to come in. He opened the door and saw me on the floor. The water was running, and he saw the empty bottles in the sink.

"What did you do? What did you do?" He was hysterically crying. I had never seen him cry this way, and I stared, mesmerized. He pulled me up, dragged me to the living room, laid me on the futon, and called 911.

He kept yelling and wailing, "Why did you do this? Why did you do this?" I remember his swollen, red face floating in front of me. For once, I had nothing to say.

When I looked up next, the police were there asking me questions. I put my hands over my ears and closed my eyes. The paramedics came and loaded me into an ambulance. The lights were flashing, and people had gathered on the street to watch.

The upside down face of a woman loomed over me in the ambulance as the doors slammed shut. "You're so stupid," she said, shaking her head.

Chapter 25:

5150

L ater that night, the ER doctor came in with a big plastic bag full of the pill bottles the police collected from my apartment.

"With the amount you took and the mixture you took, I would not have been able to revive you had you been brought into my emergency room fifteen minutes later."

My throat stung from the tube they used to pump my stomach and the taste of charcoal coated my mouth. I swallowed over the sting and asked, "When can I leave?"

He raised his eyebrows. "You won't be leaving until you pass the psych consult."

"Then go get the person I need to talk to, so I can pass it."

"It's the middle of the night, and no one is going to be able to do it until morning. You're not leaving without it because you forfeited all your rights as a human being when you tried to kill yourself." He turned and walked away.

After untangling and yanking out all the lines stuck in my body, I retrieved my clothes from the plastic bag under my cot and put on the shorts, flannel, and tennis shoes that I was wearing when I overdosed. I walked out of the room and out of the hospital. In front of the ER, I bummed a smoke off a guy and headed back to campus. It was the middle of winter, and I was a mile and a half from my apartment.

Chapter 26:

After the Storm

I stumbled into our apartment with a raging headache and hands that were bloodless, white from the cold. I banged around looking for cigarettes to smoke and didn't say anything to Theo. He gave me a half angry, half wounded look before locking himself in the bedroom. I sat on the couch smoking, trying to decide my next move. At 7 a.m., I called Grace and told her what happened. She told me to go to a meeting and tell the group. I didn't know what else to do, so I went to a meeting and told a room full of strangers that I was fresh off a suicide attempt and wished it would have worked. People tried to console me, and I ugly cried in their faces.

Theo avoided me by spending all his time with his new girlfriend. When we did cross paths, he couldn't even look at me. Other than people at meetings, who I hated, I had nobody left. I grabbed Theo by the arm one day as he was walking out and I was walking in. He screamed in my face that his girlfriend's little sister died in a tragic car accident the week earlier, and he didn't have space to deal with my selfishness. "It's not fair," I said. "She wanted to live, and I don't. It should have been me." His face went from shock and rage to resignation and disgust. He opened his mouth to say something then closed it. He wrenched his arm away from me and walked out, slamming the door behind him.

I broke down and called my mom. I'd been avoiding her because I knew she'd been happy when I had that brief stint of sobriety. But by now, she would have gotten the bill for my ambulance trip to the ER and my stomach pumping. I called without knowing what to say, just knowing I needed to hear the voice of someone who loved me.

"Carly, I am done cleaning up your messes. The way you are living your life is bringing me to my knees more than anything ever has. It's killing me to watch you." She hadn't even said hello.

"I know. I'm sorry."

"I got a call from insurance about your ambulance bill. I am not going to help you anymore if you continue on this destructive path." I heard the difference in her voice. She was serious. I'd finally worn even my own mother out.

I saw it then, how we switched seats. She went from the dying alcoholic and drug addict to the sober, caring mother. I went from the responsible, caring daughter to the dying alcoholic and drug addict. She spent the first seven years of her sobriety watching me spiral down. She endured me calling her more than once and telling her how much I wanted to die. Now, she had to contend with the real possibility that I would. And by my own hand.

But she had built an army of people in those seven years who supported and loved her as she watched me destroy myself. It was her support system that, ultimately, convinced her to give me the greatest boundary I would ever know. I can't fathom how much fear she must've had in her heart when she told me in that last phone call, "I can't help you anymore." I don't know what it took for her to say those words. The words that would eventually put me on the path to finding my own way.

My parents ended the cycle of generations of alcoholism and addiction on both sides of our family. And because of that brave choice, I would eventually become the first sober mother in all of my lineage.

In those beginning months, I fought anyone who directed me to the real work it would take to recover. I did everything I could possibly do in meetings except follow those directions. I learned the lingo of recovery, so if someone asked me how I was, I would answer back with a nod. "Taking it one day at a time." I got responsibilities to be the cookie person or the door greeter, and I fake smiled in sobriety the same way I did in the depths of my addiction. I wanted to be acknowledged for how active and busy I was, but after each long night of setting up chairs and cleaning up coffee pots at meetings, I thought about how much I still wanted to kill myself.

It wasn't until I realized I was just as hopeless and angry and destroyed in sobriety as I was when I was using that I was finally willing to listen and do what needed to be done. I met a woman named Vanessa who was beautiful with her intensely awake, sparkling eyes and her unwillingness to speak anything other than the absolute truth from her soul. She cornered me at a meeting after she saw me shifting in my chair and could tell I was trying to come up with a plan to leave early.

She held me against the wall, and got really close to my face, and told me, "Listen, I know what it feels like to be here and to want out. I see you wanting out. I also see a woman who wants to be free. I think you actually want to change. You just have no idea how that's possible. But I can see it in your eyes. You can do this."

No one had ever referred to me as a woman before. And I couldn't understand how she saw something in my eyes that was telling her I actually wanted this, that I could do this. Her conviction made me almost believe her.

But I was also still in a party town, hanging out with the same people who were doing keg stands and getting high, and I would find myself all dressed up at parties trying to convince myself that being sober was cool. And because I wasn't doing anything to change my insides, to unblock the hallway between me and God and me and the world, I was not able to be with those people and feel solid in my sobriety.

I finished the semester in Athens then went back home to Cleveland. I knew I couldn't stay sober there in that environment. My mom was willing to let me move back home temporarily on the condition that I went to meetings and stayed sober.

Back home, I found someone to help me begin to do the real work of changing. There was so much work to be done. I had barricaded myself inside myself. Where I was trapped felt like a small, smoky room full of death and despair inside of a burning building. The hallway outside was cluttered with overstuffed boxes and broken furniture. Getting sober didn't free me from that room. I had to clear the hallway between myself and myself and myself and the world. And ultimately, myself and God.

Dear Mom,

> I am so lucky the universe picked you to be my mother. We have lived so many lifetimes in this one lifetime together. So many memories come flashing back, and I have trouble figuring out how to sort them. I have never known anyone who has been such a consistent cheerleader for all of my

endeavors. That is a gift that I now get to pass on to my boys: for them to know that their mom believes in them. I get to see what it must have been like for you to raise me as I watch Levi. He is my karma baby, so I guess that makes me yours. You always drop everything to help me and the boys: picking them up from school or camp, stocking their favorite snacks in your goodie pantry, taking us on trips we can't afford to go on without you and Dad. My boys live for you. And it is not just because you give them anything; it's because you have helped me raise them. I treasure every card you ever wrote to me with your words of encouragement and declarations of pride in me. We are such different people, but when I hear your words come out of my mouth or catch your guidance in my heart, I treasure the similarities that we share. The past few years have been a lesson for the baby bird (me) as the mama bird (you) pushed me out of the nest to see if I could really fly. And it turns out that I can. All those times you believed in me and allowed me to go free, I learned how to live and make my way. Isn't that the job of a mother? So, I thank you for the formidable lessons, for the constant love, and for really good genes ('cause lady, you are still turning heads, so I'm hoping that I will be doing the same down the road). But most of all, I thank you for getting sober, and starting over, and becoming the lighthouse I would need when I washed up on the shores, drowning and desperate. If you were not there with the light on, helping me find this new way of living, I don't know where any of us would be.

Chapter 27:

The Gift of Desperation

The woman who helped me finally do the work was Julie. I liked her because she had a resting bitch face and an infectious laugh.

"I'll help you if you're willing to do anything to be sober." Without looking her in the eyes (because I couldn't look anyone, including myself, in the eyes at that point), I told her, "I will do anything."

I struggled from the moment I dragged myself out of bed in the morning until the middle of the night when I couldn't sleep. My mood fluctuated nonstop, exacerbated by the side effects from the different medications my new psychiatrist put me on. I went from being a Dean's List student to someone who could barely sit still in a chair. I spent many nights sitting next to Julie in a meeting, crying, and smoking, and asking if this was ever going to get better. She said, "It will if you do the work."

The people in recovery told me I could believe in any God I wanted but that it needed to make sense to me. They asked me what I needed God to be. When I really thought about it, what I needed from God was courage because without alcohol or drugs, everything in my life felt so big and challenging, and I didn't know how to do it. But if God was courage and

God was with me, then I could use that courage to do each Sisyphean task. And this began a relationship between me and God. A God that I had begged to take me out of this world. And God never punished me or made me feel anything other than loved and taken care of.

In that burning building, I found that the only way I could get out was to clear out what was blocking me from the exit door. That hallway that I had packed with stories of my childhood, the pain I carried with me, the loneliness I felt growing up in that house, the embarrassment, the names I was called, the humiliation, the regret from choices that I knew were wrong—all of it had to come out. And Julie showed me how to do it.

With her guidance and the courage God gave me, I got into action and excavated every last garbage bag and overstuffed box. Together, we examined the contents and found everything that was blocking me from God, and from breathing, and from living. During that first major cleaning, I discovered that almost every single story of pain and anguish I carried with me was no longer serving me. It was time to grow up, acknowledge the hurt, forgive, and move forward. I had to clean up my space and all the messes I left in my wake.

The excuses I used in the past to justify grabbing a bottle or whatever was offered no longer held any water. My parents were sober seven years and were living good lives. If I wanted to blame anyone for my misery, I only had to look in the mirror. There would be years and miles of healing ahead of me, but this was going to be on me.

From that point on, keeping the hallway clean between me and God would be my responsibility. And it would be my responsibility to get off the couch and clean up the mess.

How I saw everything changed. This new perspective was the single greatest tool I would be given. My life was my responsibility. I couldn't change what happened when I was a little girl, but I could make choices as a young woman that would set me on a new path. But none of it would be comfortable or easy.

My relationship with my mom was better than ever because I stopped complaining to her and started connecting and spending time with her. One new girl asked me to help her and then another. Julie was right. All I had to do was read from that book and share with the new girl what I was doing. I still was, very much, a mess in many areas, but I felt God within me in the most profound way I had ever known. For the first time in my life, I no longer wanted to die. I grew up. I had to.

When I was two years sober, one of the women I was mentoring through the book Julie had taken me through stood up in a meeting and said, "Carly is the woman in the rooms that girls go to when they're finally out of plans." I became a woman who would lead others through cleaning out their own hallways. And I could only do it because I knew what it was like to hate everything about yourself and be at the end of the road. I started seeing the beauty in God's world.

Once I experienced moments of beauty and peace, I wanted more.

Chapter 28:

Finding My Footing

Sober and back in Cleveland, I got a job, my own apartment, and successfully auditioned for an improv school where I discovered that I was even better at acting while sober. It made me want to get back to my unfinished degree. I transferred my transcripts from OU to Cleveland State University, a school close to my apartment and job. But the administrator at CSU told me that my two years of theater, dance, and English courses at OU would only amount to the equivalent of one year at CSU.

I was deflated and ready to give up. I stopped at the undergraduate school counseling center and was directed to find a place called First College and to talk to a professor named Paula Bloch. I walked into Paula Bloch's office with a face freshly covered in tears. Her office was small but filled with light. Books lined every possible surface. She was a tiny, fragile-looking woman.

"The counseling center told me to come find you to help me. Admissions is telling me only half of my courses from OU will count towards transfers. They're telling me I'm the equivalent of an entering sophomore."

She did not match my emotional upset. She calmly told me, "Why don't you sit down, and we will see what we can figure out together." Paula moved a stack of files from the only other chair in the room, and I sat down, handing her my crumpled transcripts.

After a few minutes, she nodded her head and said, "Well Carly, I think we can take the theater and English classes and place you into First College, where you can design your own major."

I was intrigued. "What is First College, and how do I design my own major?"

She explained that it was a small college within the larger university, where dedicated professors from every subject taught their favorite courses to First College students. I could choose three subjects to focus on and write a dissertation to defend my self-designed major. It was perfect. Paula was instrumental in helping to shape my views as a woman and as a writer. If it wasn't for her, I don't know that I would have followed through with going back to school.

The first day of classes, I sat in the front row with my fresh notebook, buzzing with gratitude. In my Death and Dying course I heard the professor recite, "Wear death on your shoulder." I had, and I never wanted to forget the bathroom floor I came from. I was excited and ready to learn, and it was clear that the professors in all of my classes were going to be incredible guides. I soaked up every word.

I took all the credits from OU that could transfer and married them with my self-designed major, The Study of the Search: The Search for Meaning. I pulled from literature, theology, and theater to show how, in all areas of life, we are searching for meaning, but we do it in a variety of ways. I heard a speaker talk about how no matter what your monument or grave marker looks like after you die, whether it is elaborate because you were wealthy or a flat, nondescript marker, all graves have one thing in common: there is a year the person was born, the year they died, and a dash between. The speaker said, "That dash is your life. That two-inch dash in between your birth year and death year is your life. What do you want to do with your dash?"

All the classes I signed up for were about philosophy, and theology, and spirituality, and feminism, and poetry. I wanted to disappear into this new world. I was hungry to learn and become. I was ready to let go of the darkness. Dr. Royster, a man with a gentle voice who looked like Santa Claus without the big belly or red suit, was one of my professors. I filled journal after journal with notes and questions about what he taught—Buddhism, Death and Dying, and Rumi.

I studied literature that spoke to my soul. I found teachers and inspiration all around me. My new professors at CSU lit a spark within me that gave the world a new hue. I read poetry that made me want to stay alive. During breaks from school, I traveled sober and saw the whole United States. I learned how to meditate, so I could download things from God. Eventually, three important messages came. First, I was always going to be okay. Second, I had to get up and keep going. And third, God was always going to be with me. I felt that.

On the day of my graduation, I had a moment with God. I walked across the stage and received an award that I wasn't even aware I earned: I graduated *magna cum laude*. In that moment, I saw what I had almost missed. Tears stung my eyes, and I said to God, "I almost missed this. Thank you."

My relationship with my mom continued to grow stronger. She was my inspiration and confidant. My relationship with my dad grew slowly but surely as well, as we had meals together, and got to know each other, and even started to like each other. I worked really hard to make right as many wrongs as I could in my life. My relationship with myself improved, and I started to understand that I deserved a good life. This led to taking myself on a solo trip across the world to Israel that transformed me even more.

Dear Dr. Royster,

I believe the universe chose you to be my professor exactly when I needed you to shine light on all the places I was not willing to look. My first semester after I transferred, I found myself in your Religion and Spirituality class, and I was ready. I was hungry and feasted on every mind-bending idea and concept you shared. You were gentle and awake. You challenged the seeker within me to dig into the readings of religions I had previously wanted nothing to do with because you knew that beauty and truth were available in places I had long ago written off as not for me. Our class came out to your farm to do meditation walks and one-on-one work with you, and from that, I experienced a very clear message from the universe. It was directly from what I believe to be my God. In meditation, I was told, "Everything is going to be OK. You have to get up and keep moving." One of the greatest gifts you gave me was asking me to participate in an independent study project where you forced me to face, within myself, truths I did not want to see and ones I didn't even know existed. On my second visit back out to your farm, with the following year's class, you pointed out how I'd changed from the year before. You said that before, I was not able to look anyone in the eye when I spoke. And now, you noticed that I connected with each person who spoke to me. You were instrumental in kindling my spiritual evolution. I know you would be proud of the woman I have grown into from the foundation of seeking that you inspired in me.

Chapter 29:

God and a Backpack

I was exhausted from school, meetings, and working as a waitress, and I hungered for an adventure. In my overfilled day planner, I had this chunk of time and in big letters I scribbled, *Go somewhere!*

After much planning and lots of God putting opportunities in my path, I had tickets to Germany and then Israel. I wanted a retreat from my regular world, like people I'd only read about. I wanted to lose myself to find myself. I was ready. My mom supported me because she knew I had to go out into the world. But my dad did not. He was constantly cutting out articles about the unrest in Israel and how dangerous it was.

I responded, "Dad, I've got God. I'm all good." He rolled his eyes as I marched off to borrow his hiking backpack for my trip.

The Sbarro pizzeria bombing in the middle of Tel Aviv (right where I planned on staying) was all over the news and my response was, "If you only watch the news, everywhere is unsafe." I was not afraid. I had just sat at the bedside of a good friend's mother, Alice, and watched her in her last days. Watching Alice die opened up a part of my heart I had long ago closed off. The course I had taken on death and dying made it so I could look death in the face and see it as a natural part of living. I wanted to get out there and live without fearing death. This trip would be my chance.

Even still, there was this quiet thought within me that I did not admit to anyone. I could hear it only faintly say, *If you go to Israel, you will not come back.* It wasn't a feeling that I would love it so much that I would move there. It was a feeling that if I went there on this specific trip at this specific time, I would not be able to return. I had no planned place to stay, no friends there, and no idea how I would get from city to city. This unplanned aspect really excited me. It made me feel independent and empowered.

My mom drove me to the airport. She hugged me goodbye with tears in her eyes, handed me a thick envelope and said, "Do not open this until you're on the plane."

I remembered the other thick envelope she gave me in the parking lot at OU. She always gave me such beautiful cards.

"Carly, I want you to promise me that if it gets too dangerous in Israel that you will leave immediately and head to Europe."

"I will." I looked down when I said it.

"I mean it. Promise me." She lifted my chin and stared into my eyes.

"I promise." I had a flash forward then. I hoped I would be the kind of mother she was, one who let her children go and explore even when she was afraid. We both had faith in God, and that faith is what allowed her to let me go.

I packed the following in my extra heavy hiking bag: a new day pack, a bunch of really lightweight clothes for the notoriously hot Israel weather, *Eden Express* by Mark Vonnegut, a Lonely Planet guidebook, my journal, four Luna bars, a still really poor self-image despite my hard-won sobriety, a lot of self-hatred, a noisy mind, and a super tight yet new relationship with God.

On that trip, I was completely alone with no one to talk to. I had endless conversations with myself and started to enjoy my own company. Back in Athens, being alone had been pure hell. It had taken so much inside work to get to the place where being alone wasn't drowning in isolation but basking in solitude.

As I traveled, the bombings in Israel continued, and the news coverage kept finding me. To calm myself, I wrote out conversations with God in my journal. I wrote, *Is this safe? Will I make it back out?* God wrote, *You're more than safe. This trip is your opportunity for us to be together. Just you and me. We can talk and listen all day long. I can answer questions you are ready to untangle. I will put people in your path to help you figure out your way. You are ready. Enjoy it!*

But as I got closer, I was afraid. From Germany, I called my dad. He was frantic. "Carly, the United States just released a statement that travelers should not go to Israel at this time." I assured him I would find out more before I went. I asked God to guide me. I asked women who were in line for a flight to Israel if it was safe to go.

One woman said, "Only Eilat is safe now." This was the only part of Israel that was nothing like Israel. It was touristy and hot, 120 degrees. It wasn't my first choice, but to minimize the risk to my life, that's where I headed. On my flight to Israel, I opened my mom's card. Written on the inside of the card was, *Fear not, for I am with you.* She ended with, *I love you. I am with you, and I respect you.* My mom had never even sat in a restaurant alone. I was more like my grandmothers in this way than like my mom, and I suspected that her respect for me was an extension of her respect for them.

A twelve-year-old Israeli girl named Naomi sat next to me. I turned to her with my Lonely Planet map opened and asked,

"Where is safe to go?" Her parents sat in front of us, and they turned to see who was talking to their child. I smiled at them and pulled my Star of David necklace out from under my shirt, so they would know I was safe. I pointed to each major city on the map, and as my fingertip covered many square miles, she shook her head. Not safe.

We spoke mainly in nouns. Naomi whispered, "No bus, no coffee, no pizza, no beaches, no taxi, and no city." I had no plans and nowhere to stay, and every alarm inside me was going off. That warning thought in the back of my mind started getting louder and moving forward: *You will not be returning from this trip.* And that warning was absolutely right—I would not be returning from that trip. I just didn't understand what that meant at the time. Removing all that crap from my hallway reaped real benefits. I heard a voice inside that guided me. Just like when I lay dying on that bathroom floor, God's voice told me that something was wrong.

The plane landed at 4:40 a.m. We unloaded onto the tarmac and loaded into a bus that sent us trembling to the terminal. The air in Tel Aviv was thick and dark. I hadn't slept in a bed in two days. I hadn't eaten a meal since I was in Cleveland. I tried asking more questions, but people in the airport refused to talk to me. No one trusted anyone. The feeling in the air was frenetic and blaring. I heard Israeli accented English, and Hebrew, and Yiddish, but couldn't understand any of it. When the beautiful and dark Israeli customs agent asked for my passport, I handed it to her looking like a terrified puppy. She asked me the same questions the agents in Germany asked me: "Where are you staying in Israel?"

"I don't know."

"Who do you know in Israel?"

"No one."

"What do you plan on doing in Israel?"

"I don't know."

"Why are you, here, in Israel?"

This last question brought the sorrow, unexpected. If I opened my mouth to speak again, to say, again, the words "I don't know," I would wail. I clamped my mouth closed and bolstered the emotional dam, holding the tears back, unwilling to openly weep at her. There was a long, silent moment between us, and then she gave me my passport and waved me through. I staggered through into Israel.

Newspapers lined shelves of little storefronts with headlines in Hebrew I didn't understand, but the pictures were unmistakable warnings: the ravaged aftermath of bombed buildings and corpses covered in sheets. My outfit, that I'd lived in for days, was sweat-soaked. My fear grew to unacceptable proportions, and I approached the airline counter to see about getting a ticket back out of there without stepping foot from the airport. I told myself that if the woman behind the ticket counter allowed me to get a return flight and the fee was no more than $75, I would leave Israel. The agent spoke English, and I explained my struggle. She told me, "I understand you want to be back with your family. There is a flight leaving for Frankfurt in three hours, no charge." She handed me my new ticket. I could finally breathe.

I went into the bathroom, and changed my clothes, and put on my sandals. After I brushed my teeth, I felt like a new human. When I headed towards my new gate, I saw the longest line I have ever seen. It was the customs line to get out of the country. Hundreds of young people were exiting, myself among them. I needed to find somewhere to go. I'd only packed clothing for hot weather. I asked a wayward teenager where I could go on a train from Frankfurt that was warm and she said, "Go to Nice!"

I decided her words were a divine directive, and several hours later, I found myself in a hotel in France having the best shower of my life. From there, I went to a beach where women lounged topless, and children were as naked and free as I finally felt. The enthusiasm with which I removed my clothes was unrepeatable.

Being alone for so many days with absolutely no one else to speak to brought clarity. I realized that the cutting words and the constant self-judgment were really just a tape on a loop. The loop brought me back to the same bullshit I would say to myself throughout my adolescence, into wayward adulthood, and straight to my would-be grave. There, topless on a beach in Nice, I had this moment—a Wizard of Oz moment— where I looked behind the curtain in my psyche only to find a tape recorder playing my lame-ass loop of self-rejection.

It was a revelation and the beginning of the journey on the road to who I am today.

That first night in Nice, showered and well-fed on *poulet fermier*, I sat in front of the long mirror in my hotel room and had the best conversation with myself of my life. That night, I made amends to the nine-year-old Carly who wanted to die and felt so alone. I talked to the teenaged Carly who never thought she was enough. I apologized for starving myself. I apologized for all the mean things I said to myself. I cried and laughed out loud, and I promised the Carly that was becoming, "I will be your best friend. I will never leave you, and I will have your back. I will be what you have always needed. I promise."

And I would need myself on that journey because traveling solo in a foreign country is lonely and frightening. I became completely aware, after listening to my own mind on a loop, that insanity and depression are a default state for me, and I could deliberately choose something else. I discovered through writing in my journal that I actually do enjoy connecting with other humans, and I made a decision to be more open and trusting with my heart, and I realized that even if I do get hurt, that guiding voice of God will always be there for me.

I wrote, *I am becoming my own best friend. I am becoming beautiful and lovable. I am becoming an extension of every man and woman who held the light in front of me to show me the way out of the cold darkness. This is living. I have already died. Now, today, this moment, this drop I savor, I shall live. I am learning to fly.*

By the time I flew back to the States, I felt changed. I even looked different. I caught a glimpse of my reflection in the tiny screen on the seat in front of me, and I actually liked what I saw. That voice inside was right. I was not returning home from that trip the same person. The Carly that arrived there a week prior was gone. Like so many, I needed to go away in order to come back to myself. I needed to face what I had been running from for all those years. I found my best friend. I met the one person who will always have my back. I became the one who will always step up for me when I need it. I only had to look in the mirror.

Dear ice cream store lady in Nice, France,

Thank you for being so awful at customer service. You were probably tired from all the tourists in and out of your shop, and so you yelled at me when

it was my turn to order ice cream. You handed
me the wrong flavor. I was traveling alone and
unexpectedly ended up in Nice instead of Israel. I
didn't speak your language and for that, I apologize.
But what I want to thank you for more is what
happened after you gave me the wrong flavor. You
see, I had just taken an amazing summer course
about women in literature, and there was a poem
called "Girl" by Jamaica Kincaid. And the gist of it
was the mama and the grandma didn't want their
girl to grow up to become the kind of woman who
would accept anything less than the best cut of
meat from the butcher. And as I stood there with
my quickly melting wrong flavor, I knew that if
I didn't go back and ask for the right ice cream
(cut of meat) I would be the kind of woman who
always accepted whatever she was given. I went
back in, and in my best attempt at broken French,
I asked for the right flavor. You were not too happy
with me, but that was fine because I walked out
with what I paid for and knew I deserved. Being
in customer service myself, I know there are many
ways to go about getting what you need, and I
only use one: respectfully and kindly asking for
what I need. And because of you, the lady in Nice,
I have never looked back. Thank you for changing
everything.

Seconds and Inches - a Memoir

Chapter 30:

Daddy Issues

Sobriety had completely transformed my relationship with my mother. I rarely spoke of my childhood to her because I never wanted her to feel pain or guilt when hearing me describe what it was like. If ever I did speak about it, it was as though I was talking about someone else's mom, so drastically had sobriety transformed her. And as close as my mom and I had become, my father and I were as far apart. Our only connection was my mom. Whenever I heard other women my age talking about how close they were with their fathers, I felt a cramp in my heart. I never had that, and sobriety hadn't given me my father. While my dad had always supported me financially and loved me because I was his child, we had never taken the time to get to know each other as human beings.

I was complaining about our lack of relationship to one of the women I worked with who said, "Why don't you have dinner together and tell him how you feel?"

I always know something is a good idea when my initial reaction is, "No way."

She smiled.

"I have never had one meal with my father, just the two of us."

"Never?"

"Nope, my mom has always been our mediator." The women around me told me that if I ever wanted to have a solid relationship with my dad, I would have to be the one to make the effort. I called him, and as shocked as he was about the invitation, he agreed to meet with me.

We met at Jimmy O'Neil's, a restaurant down the street from his pharmacy, and sat at a two-top in a dark corner. After the waiter took our orders, my dad asked, "Why'd you want to have dinner with me?"

Because I was so uncomfortable, I looked at my folded hands on the table instead of his face and said, "I feel like I don't know you, and you don't know me, and we're both sober. I think it's such a waste to not take advantage of this opportunity." I looked up.

For the first time in my life, I saw my dad tear up. "You know, I stood above Papa Bernie's grave and said to him that I wished he knew me and I knew him. I don't want you to have to do that." My heart picked up pace. With unrealistic ambition, I suggested, "Why don't we have dinner once a week?"

And because he was more grounded in reality, he countered, "How about once a month? That way, we can actually follow through." And we did. Every month, I called him and set up our dinner or breakfast date. In the beginning, it was awkward. I had to think ahead of time of topics to discuss because without my mom, we were lost. About three months in, I started to actually like the guy. We laughed and realized we had similar sarcastic senses of humor. The visits went smoother and felt easier.

About seven visits in, I was in a funk, unrelated to my relationship with my dad. It was mostly boy-related. I was having a ton of trouble feeling connected to God. But it was time to reach out to my dad to set up our meal together. We met at Tommy's, one of my favorite hippy restaurants we had been going to since I was a little girl. We sat in the back, me with my iced tea and tuna sandwich, him with his baba and falafel. The conversation was just a regular back-and-forth about school and work. Right after the waitress took our plates away, he grabbed his wallet, and I noticed his hands were shaking. He looked at me with wet eyes.

"You used to only call me when you wanted something. When you needed to borrow money or be bailed out of some trouble." He blinked and wiped the tears from his face so fast they might not have been there. His face relaxed into a resolve, that place of detachment from his emotions he was comfortable in. But he'd shown me the deeper, more real part of him, and I felt it. I felt God. I felt connected. I could see and hear. My dad was so used to me only coming to him for help that my desire to just spend time with him moved him to tears. And then I got it. That's how God feels. When I'm only going to God for help and not just to spend time, to grow closer, that's when I'm not feeling so connected. And that's what I was missing.

Dear Dad,

> We didn't get to spend a lot of time together in my childhood. You worked day and night, but you did carve out time to teach me how to hit a ball. All these years later, I can still hear your voice: "Keep your eye on the ball." And it works, it still works. I've heard that voice in my head not only for playing baseball, but for other challenges that felt too big. One day, you won't be here anymore, and

even though we butt heads sometimes, I will miss you and your guidance. It's no secret that the two of us struggle to find harmony. That we fight and step on each other's toes and have done so most of my life. I think of the Brian Andreas painting you and Mom gave me many years ago with the saying, "There has never been a day when I have not been proud of you, I said to my daughter, though some days I'm louder about other stuff so it's easy to miss that." This sums us up. We are both, usually, louder about other stuff, so it's easy to miss the good. I'm grateful for many of the things you have taught me. I'm grateful for the dog-with-a-bone way you attach yourself to a project, which taught me to not quit until I accomplish what I set out to do. I'm grateful for the work ethic and responsibility I learned from working in your store since I was twelve. I am truly grateful for you employing me even now, as a single mother of three, while I desperately need the job, the hours, and the opportunities you and Mom provide. When I first got sober and couldn't sleep at night, you invited me to call you in the middle of the night when I was struggling, and you weren't lying. I did call, and you answered. Thank you for all you do for my boys. We are so grateful for your presence in our life. Thank you for loving me the way I am, even when you don't agree with my tattoos, dirty mouth, and non-traditional choices. Thank you for introducing me to the rooms and for saving me a seat.

Chapter 31:

It's a Match

We both wanted the same things. Keith was thirty-two and wanted to get married. He didn't think I would be ready because I was only twenty-four, but I had wanted a real partnership my whole life. He was Jewish and from my hometown, and we both wanted to have kids. And while we were so incredibly different on almost every level, the saying goes that opposites attract. We did both love *Seinfeld,* and antiquing, and we wanted the same future.

Within eight months, we were engaged and moving to Boston, so he could take a job, and I could go to graduate school for my master's degree in education. We planned a *Father-of-the-Bride*-style wedding at The Ritz Carlton, and I was pregnant with our first son within months of our nuptials.

After I finished my degree and we had our first son, we moved back to Cleveland to be closer to our families. We bought a house with an acre of land that was still cheaper than our Boston rent. With the birth of my first son, Franklin, I felt a love that I had never experienced before. I loved my son more than I loved anyone or anything on earth. I wanted to eat his face, and smell his head, and hold him at all times, and wear him wherever I went. My mom came over every day and helped me with the baby. I was so happy.

By the time Franklin was nine months old, I was pregnant with my second son, Elijah. Elijah taught me that I could have two whole hearts outside my body. His eyes were so big and blue that strangers would stop me and ask if he was wearing contacts. I discovered that he was legally blind when I saw him put his face right up against things and say, "Light." I wanted my kids to be close in age and was pregnant with my third quickly after Elijah was crawling. My hearts multiplied to three, and I was in love with my boys.

When I was pregnant with my third, with daily morning sickness, I knew I was 100 percent done having babies. Two days after Franklin's third birthday, I delivered my third son, Levi. I went into that last C-section with a "Game Over" fake tattoo on my massive belly. With Levi's gender, we wanted to be surprised. I wouldn't even get to enjoy the surprise of finding out because his birth, like his life, was eventful.

Elijah had been taken to the NICU when he was born for respiratory distress, but I was never truly afraid. It felt, merely, like an unplanned detour. But when Levi was born, he made the same grunting noises Elijah had made that earned him an isolette (or incubator) in the NICU. The nurses said it was fine, but I wasn't so sure. Levi was rushed to the NICU. No one came to tell me what was going on, and they wouldn't let my mom back in to see me in the surgical recovery room. I was in a tremendous amount of pain.

After six hours in recovery, not seeing my new baby, and doses upon doses of pain meds, they finally sent me to a room. All I wanted was to see Levi. It had been seven hours since he was born, and I still had not seen him. On the way to the room, I cried and begged the nurse to take me to my baby. She wheeled me into the NICU where I could stare at Levi's tiny body with tubes and a bag at his mouth and machines beeping. I gazed at his little concave chest fighting so hard to breathe. It would be thirty-three hours before I could hold him. I had never felt so split with my love. Franklin and Elijah were home while I was a boarder in the hospital, so I could pump and be near Levi. My heart felt fractured. As hard as it was to watch Levi and to miss my other two sons, I never felt alone, and I never felt afraid that he wouldn't be okay. I had God, and my family, and friends, and the amazing doctors and nurses. I knew everything would be okay.

I was now the mother of a newborn, a nineteen-month-old, and a three-year-old. Two were in diapers and one was just learning how to use the potty. Starbucks runs were a necessity, not optional. And when a sweet, well-meaning older woman came up to me, squeezed my arm, and remarked, "These are the best years of your life," as Franklin was going boneless on the ground, Elijah was having a tantrum about chocolate milk, and Levi was having a diaper blowout, I prayed that she was wrong.

For a long time, I was happy in certain ways. On the outside, my life looked perfect. But Keith pursued another degree for a promotion at work, and he was either studying or working all the time. For more than a year, since we had Elijah and Keith changed jobs and had to study and work endless hours, I couldn't reconnect with him, no matter how I tried or what I said. I was alone with our three boys, and I had an absent roommate more than a husband. His job required him to leave the house before 7 a.m. and get home just before 7 p.m. when he'd eat a quick meal, hug his three boys, and head to the basement to study for hours.

We loved each other, but we were so busy, and on the days my parents watched the boys, he liked to be outside gardening by himself. We went to my therapist on and off and talked about how lonely I felt, but nothing would change. We would just get busier with our separate lives.

Chapter 32:

Something Is Wrong

As a baby, Levi was bald with prominent blue veins snaking over his little head like a road atlas. When he cried, the veins pulsed. When he was five months old, my uncle Sandy, a cardiologist, emphatically told me I needed to have Levi looked at. He didn't like how bulgy the veins were.

Our pediatrician, Dr. Joseph, told me it was probably nothing, but he agreed to run some tests. Dr. Joseph wrote the name and number of a specialist on a Post-it note. He said, "This is a pediatric neurosurgeon." It was a gut punch.

A few days later, we met Dr. Craig at the pediatric neurology suite. As I paced in the waiting room with Levi in his carrier, I looked at the pictures and thank-you letters to the doctor on the wall and wondered if we were in the wrong place. The kids in the pictures had scars from their foreheads to the back of their necks. Google told me that Dr. Craig was one of the best pediatric neurosurgeons in the country.

Dr. Craig measured Levi's head, grunted, and unzipped his onesie. He remarked that Levi had pectus, a concave deformation in the chest, and ordered a sedated MRI. I felt my own chest tighten.

"Is that really necessary? What are you looking for in an MRI?"

"Please just ask my assistant to help you find the first possible opening. There's no time to waste." And he was gone.

I took Levi for his MRI by myself. Keith had to take a scheduled exam. My mom watched my older boys. The sedated MRI took six hours. I sat, and I paced for six hours in the waiting room, wondering what they were doing to my baby. I started getting anxious when it was taking longer than the nurses promised. My radiologist brother-in-law, Paul, was going to read the scans, but the day was coming to a close, and I wasn't going to make it to his office to drop off the CD before he left.

When Levi woke up from anesthesia, he tried to scream, but no sound came out. He had been intubated during the scans, and his voice was hoarse. When we finally left, I drove to Paul's house to have him look at the CD of scans. I fully expected him to put my mind at ease. He would look at the scans and say, "Everything looks normal. Go home and go to bed." But that's not what happened. Paul called as we were getting the boys to bed. Keith and I listened.

"Levi's brain looks really good." He paused and took a breath. I have since learned that doctors always give the best news first.

"But he is missing the posterior dorsal part of the superior sagittal. This means Levi was born without the connector to the sinus that helps the blood flow and drain from his head. The reason his head has those big and bulgy veins in the back is that his body must be rerouting the blood."

"What does that mean?" My heart quickened. I cradled the back of Levi's head in my palm. He was asleep in the carrier.

"In adults, something like this is very dangerous because it means something is wrong with the blood flow to the brain and this created a block up. This condition would be fatal in adults. But he was born with this, and it looks like the intelligence of his body just designed around it."

All I could think was, *He said fatal. He said fatal. And missing. And rerouting.* I felt sick. I gazed at the peaceful face of my sleeping baby boy.

I wrote down what he said and thanked him. I got Levi to bed and came downstairs and found Keith in his basketball clothes.

"It's not good news. Can you stay? We need to talk," I said. He gave me a pleading look.

"I'm going to be late, and I need to blow off some steam. Talk later?" He kissed my forehead and walked out the door.

I called Uncle Sandy who is also a doctor. He said he'd never heard of this condition, but he was concerned that if Levi had one venous anomaly, there might be others. He connected me with a pediatric cardiologist at the Cleveland Clinic.

The next morning, Dr. Craig called. "He has an absence of the posterior third of the sagittal sinus. The sagittal sinus is the main drain, basically. He also has a narrowing in a transverse sinus in his neck."

"What's that mean?"

"That means the vein carrying blood down to his heart is too narrow."

"Anything else?" I gripped the phone.

"There's the pectus. For that, Levi needs to see a cardiologist to check all the connections to his heart."

"What's this condition called?" I wanted to research it online.

"There's no name for this. It's a rare genetic anomaly. I've never seen the likes of it."

"What are your concerns? What can happen?"

"Possible failure of his system. There could be traffic backup like on a highway in his head. Venous hypertension is a concern. But right now, he looks good, neurologically."

"What is venous hypertension?"

"Increased pressure in the head. It can cause brain damage."

"How will I know if he has that?"

"You would notice extreme irritability and vomiting. Possibly bleeding."

I imagined myself with all three boys at Barnes & Noble: the boys playing with the trains and then Levi just starting to cry and throw up and bleed all over me.

The doctor interrupted my nightmare and said he had to get going. I was feeding Levi cereal. He looked up at me from his high chair and smiled his gummy smile.

Chapter 33:

Rare Bird

I wrote down questions like, *What happens if Levi's system fails?*
What are the long-term implications for brain development?
Will his life expectancy be normal? That last was by far the
worst one to have to write down, much less ask. I was with Levi
at the Cleveland Clinic, waiting to see Dr. Robbins, the pediatric
cardiologist. I'd taken him for an EKG and echocardiogram
and was waiting to talk to her about the results.

Dr. Robbins was a tall brunette with piled-up hair and
glasses that kept sliding down the bridge of her nose.

"Levi's heart looks great. There were no AVMs."

"What are AVMs?"

"Arteriovenous malformations. Those are abnormal
connections between arteries and veins."

"That's great news!" Relief blanketed me. His heart looked
great.

"But he has the brain issues. My advice? If his condition
is so rare, go get a second opinion. Go find the best pediatric
neurosurgeon in the country. Find the top people and send
them the scans."

"Is that acceptable in your world? Would Dr. Craig be
offended?"

"Listen, as a parent, you have to advocate for your child. No, he won't be offended. In fact, ask him who in the country he respects and send Levi's scans there."

I thanked her and shook her hand. She gave me the knowing look of a fellow mother.

"Check out CHOP or Boston. They're the best places for pediatric neurology."

"I will. Thank you." I didn't know those places, but suddenly, I was on fire to find out about them. I was on a treasure hunt and had just been given my next clue.

Chapter 34:

Somebody Help

I called Uncle Sandy before I even called Keith or my mom.

"CHOP is Children's Hospital of Philadelphia, and Boston is Children's Hospital of Boston. I have some contacts at CHOP I can call." Because he had previously practiced at Johns Hopkins and now practiced in the Philadelphia area, he knew people at CHOP that he could contact.

"What are they calling what Levi has?"

"There's no name for it. Dr. Craig said he's never seen it before. He said it's very rare."

"OK, I'm out of my comfort zone with this. I'll reach out to some people at CHOP who can look at his scans, and I'll call you back."

In line at the hospital Starbucks, Levi was asleep in the stroller. I stared at all the doctors in line in their scrubs. I had an urge to make an announcement about Levi. I wanted them to put down their phones and help me. Briefly, I wondered if everyone was being overly dramatic and silly. I looked around expecting someone to shake me and tell me to stop all this fuss and go home, "Your kid is fine." But there wasn't time to spend wishing it weren't true. I had to get to work.

I sent out a mass text to a bunch of people I knew even remotely associated to the medical professions: *I need to find*

the best pediatric neurosurgeon in the country. That little stone
I threw in the pond caused a wave of ripples that surprised
even me. By the time I got the car from the valet, my cell was
loaded with messages and names and numbers of people who
knew people to contact.

My journal became a logbook of names: doctors and
radiologists who were willing to look at Levi's scans. I found
and contacted all the best pediatric neurosurgeons at the top
hospitals in the country. My phone became permanently
attached to my hand. The thought crossed my mind that
this couldn't have happened to a better mother. If something
needed to get done, I was the woman to do it, and I would
not accept no for an answer, especially when it concerned one
of my babies.

After that initial text, while I was walking to the valet, friends
and family started emailing and calling with specialists they
knew who wanted to help. One friend emailed that she had
just received the news about Levi and happened to be standing
in line while waiting for prescriptions next to an acquaintance
whose brother was the head pediatric neurosurgeon at one of
the top children's hospitals. He would be happy to read Levi's
scans. Another friend texted that she had recently eaten Shabbat
dinner next to a vascular surgeon at the Cleveland Clinic.

Nothing surprised me. I'd grown used to God working like
that in my life. I felt the help coming in, and I allowed it.
I had no choice. This was way beyond the work of a single
person. I needed people and connections and an audience to
help my baby. And though the help buoyed me, the fear had
unprecedented depths.

Children's Hospital of Philadelphia, Boston Children's,
and Johns Hopkins were the hospitals that came up again and

again. I sent out emails to those three and nine other pediatric neurosurgeons all over the country. These men and women were the best in their field.

Subject: Missing Sagittal Sinus

I am writing as a possible shot in the dark . . .

My son, Levi (six months), was just diagnosed as having an absence of the posterior third of the sagittal sinus.

Our neurosurgeon said he has never seen this, and it is so rare that there isn't even a Latin name for it. Have you ever encountered this?

If you could get back to me in between brain surgeries, that would be a lifesaver!

Carly

My mom left for Israel soon after. She was, is, and has always been my right hand, my fairy godmother. And she was leaving. She didn't want to leave us. I told her to go. She was tired from all the extra time she spent watching Franklin and Elijah, so I could focus on Levi, and she had really wanted to go on this trip. I would have felt awful if she stayed. I told her she had to go, and she had to let other people help me. I had a lot of work to do.

Doctors responded to my email. One early reply was from a pediatric neuroradiologist at Boston Children's:

It is unusual, and I'm not sure I've specifically seen the absence of part of the superior sagittal sinus (SSS). It's quite common to see the absence of one of the transverse sinuses, though, as there are two of them, and they divide up the work of delivering the venous blood from the brain. Sometimes, children have a developmental defect where a prominent vein leaves the SSS and travels through the bone into the scalp soft tissues, and that's called sinus pericranii, *which may be the Latin name the pediatric neurosurgeon was alluding to. Anyway, not sure if this answers your question at all.*

I looked up *sinus pericranii* and forwarded the information to Paul and Sandy. I kept a spreadsheet to organize and track correspondence sent and received. There was a huge sense of urgency. I checked my email every few minutes. My phone sat just outside of the shower, in case a doctor called. It laid on the magazine tray while I pounded the StairMaster.

It was becoming clearer that Boston was the number one children's hospital.

Dr. Simon, a pediatric neurointerventional radiologist from Boston, responded:

Absence of part of the superior sagittal sinus can just be an anatomical variant with no clinical importance to the patient, or it may result from a clot in the sinus, and it is important to separate between these possibilities. I'd be happy to look at the scans that you have if you are able to send us the CD. If so, please be in touch with my assistant by email to arrange to send that to us. In the meantime, I'd be happy to talk by phone if you forward me a contact number.

Hope bubbled up from the depths of my fear.

Chapter 35:
Advocate

Angiogram became another one of those floating words in my head. I didn't know what collateral vessels were. I found out that an angiogram was an invasive diagnostic test they could use to determine Levi's blood flow in his brain.

Dr. Joseph called me. His brother worked at Boston Children's. He told me about the angiogram and that it was risky. "Levi will need another MRI in about six months to see if his condition has changed. An angiogram requires more sedation, which isn't good for an infant."

Dr. Joseph and Uncle Sandy were the two doctors I trusted with Levi's life. What they told me became my treasure map. I needed them to hold Levi's life in their capable, do no harm hands. Dr. Joseph emphasized that looking for more information was definitely worth the effort.

Emails continued to pour in. My phone vibrated constantly with calls and texts. Keith and I barely spoke to each other. We each had to explain Levi's condition over and over again to different people.

Aunt Debra called with some amazing news: Johns Hopkins had an entire pediatric neurology team made up of interventional neuroradiologists, vascular neurologists, and neurosurgeons that was going to sit down and look at Levi's case that Thursday. I had to get them the CD with his scans by Tuesday. They mentioned to Debra and Sandy that there was possibly a noninvasive (nonsurgical) approach to solve Levi's problem. More hope bubbled up around my head, held just barely above water.

Chapter 36:

Get in the Barrel

W hile I waited for the news from the team at Johns Hopkins, I had a sense that I wasn't being told the whole story about Levi. It seemed to me that doctors, and my family, and my friends were trying to protect me from some terrible truth. I had done it. I had withheld important information that might be challenging for someone to hear because I thought I'd spare them some pain. I had done it to the people I love.

One of my close friends told me a parable about faith. There's a stunt performer standing at the edge of a cliff with a barrel and a high wire stretched across an abyss. The performer is surrounded by a crowd of onlookers. He challenges the crowd and points to a man. "Excuse me, sir, you see this barrel?" The man nods.

"Do you think if I get in this barrel and try to make it across this wire, I could?"

The man looks at the others around him, smiles, and says, "Yeah, I guess. I believe it."

The performer says, "So you believe I can do it? You believe if I get in this barrel, I can make it across this wire without falling?"

The man shrugs, and laughs, and says, "Yeah, I believe you can do it."

The performer gets in the barrel and is given a great big push by his assistant. Across the wire and back he goes. When he comes back, he walks up to the same man and bows. He then says, "You believed I could do it. But do you have faith that it can be done?"

The man says, "Yeah, I have faith it can be done."

The performer pushes the man towards the edge of the cliff and says, "If you have faith, then get in the barrel."

The difference between belief and faith only becomes clear when you have to get in the barrel.

The one thing I was certain about since getting sober was my belief in God. After years in sobriety, searching and trudging through all that blocked me from a true relationship with God, I had found my own conception of God. We were best friends. I knew I could count on God for anything. But I had a Disneyland kind of God.

With the God I used to believe in, everything that happened in my life happened for a reason. Disneyland God had a plan, and it would all work out the way it was supposed to work out. If a situation didn't work out a certain way, then it wasn't Disneyland God's plan. If it did, then it was. If I got a speeding ticket, it was Disneyland God's will for me to have been stopped, so I would miss an oncoming accident further down the road. If we missed a flight, then that was Disneyland God's plan, because I might have needed to be in the terminal at a specific time to bump into someone I needed to meet.

It was blind, blind belief untested by faith, and I loved it. I'm sure it bothered the people around me who might not have been as open to the will of God as I was, like Keith. But I went forth with my beliefs and apologized to no one. It was almost foolproof. Almost.

Events like the Holocaust and slavery stood in the way of making this belief foolproof, but I worked around it by attributing such atrocities to the free will of humans. The way I understood it was that God gave us free will, and God could not stop a person from using their own will. I didn't like it, but it wasn't God's fault. Then, a few life events knocked me off my perch of certainty. When a good friend of mine was looking at a gun at his buddy's house and accidentally shot himself in the head, dead at twenty-nine, that was a kick to the spiritual stomach. Then my dad's younger brother, beloved Uncle Evan, was diagnosed with a horrific form of brain cancer and died in agonizing pain, leaving two kids and a lot of questions. I was pissed off.

What I came up with was that horrible events happen in this world, and I might never understand them, but I do need to believe that God knows what He's doing. And that was that.

But then the universe asked me to get in the barrel.

These were my prayers each morning as I was jarred back to reality when Levi was finally asleep, Franklin was climbing into bed to snuggle, and Elijah was screaming in his crib because he couldn't get out: "God, please give me the strength and courage to get through today." My prayers were so simple and so immediate. Normally I asked for help to be useful, and kind, and loving, but this wasn't normal. I needed courage and strength to just keep going.

I stopped praying, "Thy will be done," because I was not interested in knowing God's will in this case, nor was I interested in it being done, necessarily. This was the first time in my almost eleven years of sobriety that I stopped turning everything over to God. Not saying the words wouldn't change the outcome, but I wasn't able to fathom a world where I turned Levi's life over to God, and God took my baby, and I had to go on living without that relationship.

I knew I needed God; I just couldn't imagine how I could go to a God that thought the best outcome was to take Levi. So, my prayers became simple and constant. "Please help me get through this. Please give me whatever I need to handle the next piece of news." God answered those prayers. I felt the strength of the people all around us. I felt their prayers, and their love, and read their texts and emails. They carried me.

I also waded through the well-meant comments that cut me to my core and isolated me in my own prison. Comments like, "Everything happens for a reason." Or, "He will be fine. I just know it." The first one pissed me off because that implied that my son was suffering and potentially was going to die for a reason. The second one was worse. Because as soon as someone said it, they were cut off from me. With those well-meant words, I felt unheard. They didn't know that. They couldn't know that. They didn't know that Levi was going to be okay. No one did. So as I continued walking, I tried to gently tell the people closest to me what was helpful and what was hurtful for me to hear.

Chapter 37:

First, Do No Harm

I was still waiting for the news from the team at Johns Hopkins when one of my closest friends, Elana, introduced me to her very good friend, a neonatologist named Jacob. He became indispensable in my life. "The first thing we need to do is no harm," he said when I first met him. "Some types of intervention can cause more problems. You don't want to hurt the brain." This was scary—to hear the dangers of doing nothing, the dangers of taking action, and having to decide which course was less dangerous.

When did these choices about the quality of Levi's life become ours to make? Jacob mentioned venous hypertension again. He said the development of venous hypertension would be slow. Until then, I had imagined it would be a horrible episode that happened at 5:45 p.m. one evening while Franklin and Elijah were eating dinner, and Levi would just start screaming and vomiting. On the contrary, Jacob explained, the symptoms develop slowly, over time.

Jacob kept talking about the million-dollar question: to intervene or not to intervene? He also agreed that it was best to get other opinions from the most experienced people who didn't want to jump into any intervention. "Carly, time is of the essence. You need to be very careful with what doctors are doing to Levi. What do you think is the best course to take?"

This became the question that owned all of the space in my head. How was I supposed to know? I prayed, "God, please guide me."

More and more doctors requested Levi's scans. I sent out thirteen CDs in total. CHOP was no longer a contender given their inexperience with a case like this. Boston and Hopkins seemed to be our two main choices. I became more and more uncertain with each email and call. We were getting inundated with emails from pediatric neuro people wanting to know if Levi was experiencing any symptoms and what was going on with his development. With this line of questioning, it emerged that Levi might have had some developmental red flags for his age. Levi's head/weight/height measurements were slightly off from where they should be. He couldn't eat any baby food that wasn't pasty in consistency, couldn't sit up at all, and couldn't stay seated in a high chair. Dr. Joseph said he wouldn't be concerned about these things in a regular six-month-old but that he was with Levi. He suggested Levi have the angiogram. But Keith's brother-in-law, Paul, disagreed. And Dr. Simon from Boston Children's was on the fence, suggesting we do the angiogram only if Levi presented any concerning symptoms like the appearance of the bulging veins changing or signs of significant developmental delays.

The risks of the angiogram were that Levi's leg could stop growing at the injection site or it could cause a blood clot and stroke. But the risk of not having the angiogram was lack of information—not knowing what other venous anomalies might be present in his body—and potentially allowing something preventable to happen, like the venous hypertension, or worse.

As if tensions weren't already too high between Keith and I, we disagreed on how to move forward. He wasn't so sure about the angiogram, and I wanted Levi to have it. He hadn't been the one in communication with all the different doctors. He only had his brother-in-law, Paul's, perspective, which he considered gospel. I appreciated Paul's opinion, but I had many other voices floating around in my head. The effect was a sense of urgency to rule out more problems or treat existing problems we didn't know about yet.

When I finally heard from the team at Johns Hopkins, I was in Starbucks with all three boys. I ran into a corner and called Keith to conference him in, so he would hear this prestigious team's opinion with me. The speaker introduced himself as Dr. Taylor, the head of pediatric neurosurgery. "We think Levi should have an angiogram as soon as possible," he said.

"Can you explain why? We've had conflicting opinions," Keith said.

"There's a big unknown about how Levi's venous drainage system works, and the angiogram is the only diagnostic test that can give us that knowledge."

Levi started screaming in the stroller just as my other two boys started crawling on their hands and knees under tables and across the dirty floor of the coffee shop. I put the phone on speaker and pressed mute then whisper-shouted for them to get off the floor while picking up Levi and bouncing him in my arms. I tuned back into the call in the middle of Dr. Taylor's answer to some question Keith had asked.

"One concern with this sort of condition is an arterial venous malformation or AVM, which we'll need to rule out. We're not seeing any AVMs from Levi's scans, but if there is one, it could rupture or cause severe blood loss resulting in a condition called steal syndrome, which is very dangerous."

"I took him to see the cardiologist," I shouted, "and she said he didn't have any AVMs." My tone was defensive. I tried to take a deep breath, but the air wouldn't penetrate my lungs.

"Like I said, we're not seeing any AVMs on his scans, but the angiogram would be the only thing to definitively rule that out."

Levi was quiet, and the older two boys sat obediently in chairs beside me, sensing the turmoil now. I still had trouble getting a good breath.

"What else are you wanting to rule out," Keith asked. Gratitude for his clear, objective thinking flooded through me. These were the questions that needed to be asked, and I wasn't thinking of them.

"The most important factor is the blood flow. We could do an additional test during the angiogram with occlusion. If we are able to occlude, or close off, the venous system manually then we would be able to see how it would handle blood flow without the drainage area Levi's body created. With the sagittal sinus closed off, we want to know, is there enough of a drain? There is also venous hypertension to be aware of. The angiogram will give us a sense on how much backup there might be in the brain."

I heard a pen scratching and hoped it was Keith writing all this down. He asked, "And what treatments would you suggest if you weren't able to rule these things out?"

"With surgery, we could remove the venous drainage area Levi's body created and reroute it. If there is no AVM, we will still need to do something. In some form or another, Levi will need surgery."

With those words, I heard the gates of hell clang shut behind me.

"What kind of surgery?" I asked.

"It's a pretty simple concept. We would disconnect the vein that runs through the skull and just remove it. Then we would see if the venous drainage could be restored somehow. Maybe the sagittal sinus could be opened up. A second scenario is where we would stage a venous drainage removal in pieces. Stage one would be removing a small piece and monitoring how his system does over time and then going back in for stage and taking it down to nothing. This would require multiple surgeries."

A large, invisible vise-grip was pressing down on my body. Multiple brain surgeries. Weeks at a time in another city. Now, my hope was whittled down to my baby needing only one brain surgery.

Keith asked, "Have you seen a child with this condition before?"

The answer was the same answer we had been hearing: a resounding, "No."

I asked, "What could happen if we don't do the angiogram?"

"I don't think Levi can have a worry-free life if we don't move forward with the angiogram."

Levi, his wide, bright eyes gazing up at me from my arms, looked decidedly worry-free.

Chapter 38:

Where Shit Meets Fan

A friend asked me, "Do you know what the pediatric intensive care units are like at each hospital?" The question itself stopped me in my tracks. I should have been planning ahead and researching these things, but all I wanted was to start having the doctors give us consistent guidance. We were in limbo, and it was really uncomfortable. The not knowing is what got to me.

When I called Sandy to ask him questions he was upset. "Have you talked with Lulu?"

"No, why?"

"Papa Harry was peeing blood and was in incredible pain."

My papa never complains. They were in Florida for the winter, and I was concerned. I immediately called my mom, so, over the phone, she could help Lulu take Papa to the hospital. My mom was supposed to be coming over to watch my older two boys while I took Ruby to be rehomed. (Keith and I had decided to rehome our dog, Ruby, because having her was just too much.) The added layer of responsibility was spoken for and then some by Levi's medical crisis, and there were still the competing needs of my other two kids. All of this converged on the same morning. Now, I wouldn't have my mom's help. As I rushed around the house gathering everything for Ruby and the boys to load everybody in the car, the phone rang. It was another doctor I had emailed, and it ended up being one of the worst calls of my life.

I had emailed a doctor that my friend, Allyson, had met at Shabbat dinner and who was willing to help us find some answers. His name was Dr. Berger, and he was a vascular neurosurgeon at the Cleveland Clinic. To say Dr. Berger had no bedside manner is a euphemism at best. He talked really fast, so fast I could barely keep up in my journal with all he had to say.

"What your son has is almost unheard of. It's exquisitely rare and uncommon. But does it matter?" He paused. I felt confused. Of course it fucking matters.

"It's impossible to know. He's doing fine, and his brain looks great. It's clearly doing its job. Do you need something to be done? It's anybody's guess, but probably no, you won't need anything done. Besides, he's too small to be doing anything crazy."

I asked, "Do you think we should do an angiogram?"

"Well, you do an angiogram to get a result. I would not do an angiogram."

"Why?"

"If the result is to figure out what treatment to move ahead with, it isn't worth it. Surgery would be unbearably risky. Operating would be terrifying. At his age, he only has one liter of blood in his whole body." He then asked me the worst question anyone has ever asked me. "Do you know how many minutes it would take a seven-month-old to bleed out on the table if they made one wrong move?" My whole body went cold. It felt as though I'd just been drained of blood. I closed my eyes, and it was all I could see: my baby rapidly bleeding on the operating table.

"He can bleed out one liter of blood in five minutes on the surgical table when they open him up." My head suddenly felt terribly light, and I worried I was losing consciousness. Never in my life had I felt like I was going to faint. "There is no room for error. If they do bleed him out, it's impossible to keep up with the bleeding. The risk of death is real. It is not insignificant. The only way to do this is on cardiac standstill. And even cardiac standstill comes with intrinsic risks."

I blurted out, "What's cardiac standstill?" I wished I'd never asked.

And then he painted another picture in my mind that I will never unsee. "We have to stop Levi's heart, so the blood stops flowing, and perform the surgery with a pediatric cardiac team, an anesthesiology team, and a neurovascular team. That's *the* only way you could do it. You'd be okay with the surgery in Cleveland because of the heart team we have at the Clinic. It's the only way I'd trust to do this."

I felt dizzy from speeding, colliding thoughts. I knew that I didn't want to go to Cleveland for this procedure. I was suddenly enraged at this doctor and his gall in talking to a mother like that, graphically describing to her the gruesome death of her child. I hated him so much, I clenched my teeth and fists. It gave me momentary strength. But then as quickly as it flared up, it went away, leaving me even weaker, more terrified, and sadder than before. But feelings were an expired luxury I could no longer indulge in. I would never be able to get the picture of my baby lying on a table with his heart stopped out of my head. I would want to crawl in a hole. But I would bear the pain I was feeling and keep walking forward into whatever future he had.

I was still on the phone with Dr. Berger. His voice almost startled me. "Are you going to justify all this risk? I don't have issues with the angiogram, but you must understand that you do the angiogram with the intention of changing your management. What would I do? I'd wait until Levi gets physically larger to do *anything*. When would I do it? I wouldn't intervene until he develops venous hypertension or significant developmental delay or decline. Then I'd reconsider doing something."

"So you'd wait until he has brain bleeding and damage before you did anything?"

"Yes. The risks of taking action on a six-month-old now outweigh the potential rewards, and the risks are very real. By the time he's two years old, it becomes much safer. But, yes, you have the risk of him developing venous hypertension. Here's the question I have: what will an angiogram show me to change my decision?"

I told him, with tears in my throat, "I don't know who to listen to. I have Hopkins telling me that we need to do an angiogram and we need to do it very soon to figure out what treatment we can do. I have you telling me if we do this, it could kill him, and if we don't do anything, he could suffer a stroke. Who do I listen to?"

His response destroyed me. "Intervention could work, but at what price? How about the price of death?"

We hung up as my mom walked in the door, and I was already running late to take Ruby to her new home and Levi to his appointments. I was hysterical inside but so relieved to see her and have the help.

When I finally got there with Levi, I walked into Dr. Joseph's office and waited for his calming presence. He checked out Levi to see why he was being so fussy and found that he had an ear infection.

I told him about the call I just had, and he was visibly upset by it. He didn't like the way Dr. Berger spoke to me either. He reminded me again, "Hopkins and Boston are two of the very best teams, and you would be completely taken care of wherever you end up." I needed his reassurance.

"Both hospitals do angiograms all the time on infants, and you do need to go ahead with the angiogram. You need to stop listening to all these doctors and only listen to Hopkins and Boston."

We had three more days until we were due to hear back from Boston. I was living on coffee and nutrition bars. I felt that I was certainly developing an ulcer and was constantly on the verge of having a full-scale breakdown but was just teetering on the edge of keeping it together to take care of my kids.

We left Dr. Joseph's office and went downtown to the Cleveland Clinic to meet with Dr. Newman, the pediatric neurologist that so many had recommended. His resident spoke to us first. "What Hopkins is suggesting about occluding can be very dangerous because you don't want him to have a stroke. When they occlude the vein, it stops the blood from flowing through that area. A stroke is brain tissue damage because the brain doesn't have enough oxygen. That's the risk of doing the angiogram with the intention of occluding the venous system. If you do nothing though, the risks are stroke, and venous hypertension, or a bleed. The stroke would be sudden, and there's no way of predicting it, and the bleed would be clear by seizures, hemorrhaging, or if Levi was unresponsive or sleepy. It would be the same presentation as a stroke."

She barely took a breath. "The problem is that the brain is already taking up the entire space in the skull. We don't want Levi to bleed because then the skull has no more space to hold the blood. This is a dominant vein, and there are risks with his condition if you do something and risks if you do nothing."

I realized I was holding my breath, and I gasped for air, which startled her a bit. Dr. Newman came into the room. He was a big, burly, friendly-looking man about my father's age. He spoke with a heavy South African dialect, which I found calming.

He sat down and leaned in. "There are two separate issues here. One is the angiogram. We do the angiogram to get a better look at Levi's anatomy and to understand what is happening. The other issue is surgery. Surgery is a whole different ball game. You don't know how the blood will dissipate and where the blood will go if you occlude these veins. I don't know if Dr. Berger is so far off base with what he was saying. If it is just venous issues, are those vessels normal or abnormal? Will they rupture due to internal pressure or trauma? Potentially, the angiogram can be dangerous, but mostly, because of the occluding Hopkins is suggesting. If you go to Boston, where I did my residency, you'll be in the best hands."

Relief flooded me. Finally, I had someone who was willing to tell me where to go. The man with the calming voice gave me the two syllables that would deliver me from the paralysis of the most painful indecision of my life: Boston.

Chapter 39:

Balance Beam

Intellectually, I know God has my back, but I forget a lot. I sometimes call myself Dory, the character from the movie *Finding Dory*, because she has short-term memory loss. This is like me when it comes to God. I forget every day. I forget that there has never been a time when I didn't get what I needed, even when that wasn't what I wanted. But there has never been a time when God left me alone without the support and the resources to walk through whatever was in front of me.

When I forget, I picture myself at age six in a light pink leotard with opaque pink tights and ballet slippers. My hair is in a loose ponytail, and my tongue is sticking out in childlike concentration on my footing. I hesitantly take a step forward and then stop and look around in fear, afraid of falling.

That's when I feel God's strong hand on my shoulder and hear God's clear voice say, "I've got you." I take another slow and careful step then pause and look around, afraid again. I feel God's hand, and I hear God's voice again, "I've got you." I walk like this throughout my life. Afraid, and then with courage, and then afraid, and then with the knowledge that God is right with me.

The day I made the decision to take Levi to Boston for the angiogram, I ran upstairs and locked myself in the bathroom to call my best friend, Elana. Hysterical on the phone, she barely understood me wailing about everything I'd learned and how Levi might die but we had to take the chance or else he might also die and I'd never been more afraid or lost. I couldn't get out of my head the vision of Levi's tiny body lying silent in surgery with all those tubes and machines and doctors trying to keep him alive. I sat on the closed toilet seat and went through everything I could do to make these feelings go away. Each option—getting drunk, getting high, smoking, stealing, hurting myself, running away—was no longer on the menu for me.

"All you have left is God," Elana said. Her voice cut through my despair. All I had left was God.

Chapter 40:

Michelangelo

My mom came over to pick me up to go to a meeting, and we both looked like we hadn't slept for days. I couldn't concentrate on the speaker and had to stare at her, so if she looked my way, she would think I was paying attention. It was the first time I had ever sat in a meeting and thought how lucky these people were to only have a fatal drinking problem that could be treated with meetings and spiritual principles.

Keith and I had nothing to say to each other. Lying next to him in bed in silence every night was torture. Sleeping was torture because of the nightmares. I could not handle even one quiet moment in my head. I could not bear the thoughts that circled like vultures: *What would it be like to have only two kids again? Should I take a picture of Levi today because it might be the last chance I'll have?* The fear made me want to jump out of a window.

My parents gave me their credit card to pay for flights and hotels. We couldn't have afforded it by ourselves. We had a missing wall and a giant hole in our kitchen roof that was covered with plastic tarps. Now, the pending construction and progressive leak seemed like a footnote to real problems. I didn't know how anything was going to get done, but all I cared about was keeping my baby alive.

Levi kept having fevers in spite of the antibiotics for his ear infection. I took him back to Dr. Joseph.

Dr. Joseph took out a measuring tape and wrapped it around Levi's bald, little head. He touched and peered closely at the bulging, zagging blue veins. "Where are you on the decision of what to do?"

"We're doing the angiogram at Boston Children's," I said.

"Good. Levi's veins look significantly worse. And the ear infection is cleared, so I don't know what's causing his fevers."

While I waited to hear from Dr. Simon in Boston, I kept my phone close with its ringer on. I was used to sleeping, showering, eating, and breathing with my phone at my fingertips. One night, as Franklin drifted off to sleep beside me in his bed, I got a call from a 617 number, which I knew meant Boston from our time living in Cambridge. I snuck out of his room to answer.

Dr. Simon had received the report on the worsening of Levi's swollen veins and was concerned. He said he made space in his calendar to do the angiogram a week from that day.

"What are the potential outcomes of this test? What are the treatments you have in mind, based on what you find?"

"The first and best scenario is that Levi's system could be fixed through interventional radiation. This is my hope, but I do not think it's likely. I think the chances of Levi's venous system being fixed without a scalpel are really low."

I gripped the phone harder and felt the, now familiar, swell of nausea.

"The second scenario would be a surgical intervention. It would be the cardiac bypass surgery. In this scenario, we might monitor him and see how he does before doing the surgery."

He paused and cleared his throat.

"The worst outcome would be if we discover his system is not sufficient, and we cannot do the surgery because it is too risky."

I asked him to hold. My hand shook, and I pulled the phone away from my face. Realizing I'd been holding my breath, I exhaled. I looked around for the journal where I'd written out all my questions, but couldn't find it. I returned to the phone and thanked him. He gave me the number to his scheduler to confirm the time, and I booked our plane tickets as soon as I hung up.

I thought about the story of the artist, Michelangelo, who said he did not create the *David*, but rather he removed all that wasn't *David*. That is what happened. Instead of knowing where to go, the universe removed every place that was not where we needed to go, and Boston was just sitting there, shining on its own.

But I didn't want to go to Boston. I didn't want any of this to be happening. The fire in my chest was back. Only this time, I had to be sober. I wanted to pick up my baby, and run away, and not answer anyone's calls or emails, and pretend that he was totally fine.

But that kind of pretending was no longer an option. That was the conversation that made me realize this was all horribly real. Just a few weeks earlier, I was most concerned about leaving Franklin and Elijah, and now, my biggest hope was that they could fix my baby with the scariest surgery I had ever heard of. The pictures of him lying on that table refused to leave my head alone.

Dear Dr. Joseph,

I don't play the lottery, ever, because I actually feel like I have already won so many times over.

Because I hit the biggest lottery by finding you as our pediatrician. You are part of my parenting tribe as the doctor helping me raise these three boys. You held each of them at their first checkup and every one since. You have counseled me when I've been worried and have always been 100 percent forthright, humble, and giving in so many ways. You admit when you don't know, and you speak up when you do. I have been around more doctors than the average parent, and I can unequivocally say that you are the best doctor I have ever met. The relationship, confidence, and guidance I have received from you with Levi has been life-changing. I don't know if you ever wonder if you have made a difference in this world, but I can tell you with all of my heart, you have made a difference in our world. The day the pediatric neurosurgeon told me he had never seen another patient with the blockage Levi had and offered no help from there, after I had heard from him about how Levi's system could fail, well, I was completely adrift; but you called me after hours and told me it was my job to advocate for Levi. And you lit a fire of permission and obligation for me as his mother. And since that evening, nothing has come in between me and getting Levi what he needs. I cannot think of a more sacred relationship for raising a family than the trust and respect between an outstanding doctor and a concerned parent.

Chapter 41:

Batman Page

The burning feeling inside spread through my whole torso while I tried to book flights on my phone and figure it all out—getting to Boston with Levi, getting Franklin and Elijah covered. I couldn't do it on my own anymore. I texted my friends, Elana and Allyson, *I need help*. I so rarely asked for help even though they had been telling me they would do anything.

My parents were in Florida with Papa Harry, who was in the hospital by then, and my in-laws were visiting family in Chicago. My friends came over in minutes. I had no idea how they pulled it together so quickly, with their own little kids, but I will always be in their debt.

Elana took charge of airline tickets. Allyson entertained the boys. I asked Franklin to go in the other room and watch TV, so I could talk to my friends. I didn't want him to hear what we were saying. He was smart, and this was scary.

I finally spoke my biggest fear. "I'm so afraid of going on the plane to Boston with my baby and not coming home with him." We all cried, and hugged, and felt so powerless. There were no more words to say. My friends stayed with me and helped me make the small decisions I was no longer able to make. I asked them questions like, "Do I bring winter boots?" because I just couldn't figure it out on my own.

I kept breaking down and weeping as I packed, but Elana helped me the way I had asked her to. "You are on a mission to save your baby boy. There is no time for emotions."

A few days later, my mom came back from Florida and came over to take us to the airport. I ran around the house throwing last minute items in our suitcases, and we piled the boys in the car. My mom was my brain because I no longer had one. I was dreading saying goodbye to Franklin and Elijah, but luckily didn't have much time to think about it. We headed to pick up Keith from work and trudged through the falling snow.

When we arrived at the airport, I felt the reality of the situation slam down on me again. My mom got out to help us and gave me a huge bear hug. I broke down in her arms. I cried into her shoulder and thought of the next time I'd see her and what would become of all of us. I thought about how she could send her little girl off on such an errand without her, but I looked back at my two older boys and my littlest and knew that the girl had to become a woman, and more importantly, a mother.

I kissed Franklin and Elijah. I squeezed them so closely and took in their smells and told them, "We will see you so soon." All they knew was that we were going to take Levi to get his head fixed and the best doctors were in Boston.

It was early in the morning and the airport was almost completely empty. There were no lines. We couldn't believe our flight would be taking off with all of the snow coming down. It was so quiet in the terminal. I held Levi and looked around at the few people getting ready for a business trip or a vacation, and here we were, on our way to the most difficult thing of my life.

Keith checked his email and found one from his brother-in-law, Paul. The very doctor who had helped us so much and was the first to tell us what was going on was now turning the medical towards the spiritual. The email was forwarded after Paul sent it to his synagogue: *Gadi, below are the Hebrew names of two souls who need* Mi Shebeirach. *Seven-month-old baby Levi has a serious brain condition, and eighty-year-old Holocaust survivor Harry has cancer. Please remember them over the Torah.* Whenever someone shared that they were praying for my son, I felt overcome by emotion. In the Wailing Wall in Israel, people had put tiny pieces of paper, folded prayers for my son, to God.

The night before the angiogram, I experienced the most fear I have ever known. I just wanted Keith to hold my hand and tell me that no matter what, we would get through this together. He never did, most likely because he was just as frozen in fear as I was. Not only was the fear paralyzing, but Levi was throwing up the entire night, and we had to constantly get up and clean him and ourselves in the little hotel sink. We were panicked that the anesthesiologist wouldn't let him be sedated if they knew he was sick.

Chapter 42:

Morning Sickness

We reached out to Dr. Joseph in the early morning and asked him what we should do. If the anesthesiologist found out that he was sick, they would cancel the angiogram. Everyone agreed. He needed the angiogram. After Levi's eye pressure was checked out and confirmed to be normal, it was decided this was just bad timing for the stomach bug. I changed him and didn't nurse him because he wasn't allowed to eat and brought him to the pediatric waiting room.

Every time he started to dry heave, I rushed him into the bathroom and let him throw up in the sink. I looked in the mirror, saw how tired I was and how horrible Levi looked, and just hoped they would call us in soon. There were kids and families there with luggage, ready to move in for whatever surgery they were awaiting. There were kids with their blankies and their stuffed animals. I heard a father tell his teenaged son, "I wish I could take your place." Even with all that was ahead of us, I wondered if their fates were worse than ours. And then Levi's name was called.

The team decided to proceed with the angiogram, despite Levi's stomach bug. We were ushered to the pre-op room where we met Dr. Simon. He was young, kind, and direct. He told us that the pediatric neurovascular team had just reviewed Levi's case and confirmed that the angiogram was the next logical step. One condition they would be looking for that could cause the veins to change was an AVM. I was put at ease by the way Dr. Simon explained Levi's case. He simply told us that we would know so much more after the angiogram, and he would come and tell us the next steps right afterwards.

The nurse came to take Levi from my arms. We kissed our sweet boy goodbye, and they took him away. I watched his little face over the shoulder of a nurse as the doors to the operating area closed. There was no more work to do. I couldn't email or call any other doctors for opinions or arrange for anything else to be done. I had done all I could do, and now, my only job was to wait. Without him in my arms, I felt empty and nauseous.

We gave the nurse our mobile numbers and walked outside to Starbucks. We needed to get away from that floor. It was an entire floor designated just for family members who were waiting for their children to get out of surgery. It was bright white with the fluorescent lights and parents looking like zombies staring at the wall and empty coffee cups. I wondered briefly if the other parents were made closer by their shared tragedy. Keith and I were not a team in this storm. We did not hold hands. We were not there for each other. We were there only for our son and ourselves.

As we walked through the revolving doors, we saw a woman entering the hospital with tears all over her face. The looks on the faces of those mothers made me realize that I could never again feel comfortable with the idea that it is all God's will. I felt like I had finally seen behind the curtain, and I could no longer believe what I once had. I could not pray for God's will to be done if His will might be for children to be so sick or die so young. Something inside of me changed, and the innocent relationship I had with God was different. I wasn't angry, I just was not convinced that the God I believed in thought it was a good idea for a baby or a child to have a fatal illness or medical complication. I just didn't buy it. I concluded that this was part of life that I might never be able to comprehend.

Waiting and wondering were the worst parts. I was getting constant messages from family and friends wanting updates. I knew nothing. Keith and I barely spoke, and the silence was so loud. He clenched his jaw like he does when he is contemplating something. My knees never stopped bouncing. My chest was constricted.

In the waiting room, I noticed that the doctors gave the news right there unless it was bad news. Then they take the parents to the consult room. Several hours later, when Dr. Simon came into the waiting room and asked us to follow him to the consult room, my whole body heated up. We entered the very same room where the other mother had come out crying hours ago. Her Gatorade was still on the side table, half full. I didn't know how to hear what came next. I sat down trembling. There was a framed Picasso poster on the wall, the one with the flower vase outline. I wondered who was assigned to decorate this awful room and how they decided that vase would be what families would need when hearing news like this.

"We performed the angiogram. Levi is in recovery. His brain looks really good. This is just a venous drainage issue. No AVMs, no lesions. We saw an anomalous drainage at the site where Levi's superior sagittal sinus would be. His is not there. He has *sinus pericranii* of a crucial vein that cannot be treated or closed. Some patients with *sinus pericranii* have it in a noncrucial vein and treatment is an option, but that is not the case with Levi. He has other venous anomalies, a number of which are in areas that are not so well developed. One specific area we discovered was his torcula, which is the connecting point of the superior sagittal sinus, straight sinus, and occipital sinus. It is very underdeveloped. There is no sign of narrowing in the veins, and when we followed the flow, we found Levi's drainage goes out an alternate pathway at a normal, good flow."

My mouth fell open and I heard a sound from Keith. I glanced at him, and his mouth was open. This sounded like excellent news.

"Levi's brain found an alternative pathway to drain, and it looks good. If I had to speculate why this happened, I would say it occurred in utero. There was most likely a clotting episode, but the brain worked around it."

"So, he doesn't need surgery?" I asked. I opened my journal with all of the post-angiogram questions written in it.

"No, his venous system is good."

He paused, and I had the sense the bad news was coming next. The other shoe.

"I always like to give the best and most important news first. Levi's venous system is working for him. The downside is that it is anomalous, and we cannot treat the system or close the veins."

Keith searched around for his voice, stuttered a bit, then asked, "Is treatment not a viable option because there isn't anything you can do to fix this or because nothing needs to be fixed?" I was grateful that he was able to pull it together and focus in that stifling room.

"Levi's system is totally sufficient, and I do not see any reason for this to affect development. There is no pressure issue or concern of venous hypertension. The developmental concerns and delays you have noticed are unrelated to his brain or venous system."

I asked, "Why are his veins becoming so prominent? Will they continue to be?"

"They should not grow too much more beyond his first year, and that's just a cosmetic concern. I don't have a good answer for why they have become so much more prominent recently, but they could possibly continue to grow down Levi's face. In that case, they would always be there."

The doctor glanced at his watch and then the door. I felt like time was running out and had to scan through my list of questions to the really important ones. The letters and words blurred together on the page. I asked, "What's the next step? Are we waiting and watching? And what are we watching for?"

"We don't want the veins to close, as that would be very dangerous and result in bleeding or strokes. Levi will have scans in six months and yearly after that. If he has two years of good scans, he can stop. We would see signs of closing in the scans by then."

I asked, "How would we know from the outside if the veins are closing?"

"Hard to tell. It could be a very drastic change in the appearance of his veins, meaning they might become way more prominent or they might start to disappear. The crucial time to watch is over the next year as the bones in his head grow together. The bones moving closer in could cause a problem. After Levi turns one, we could remove bones to prevent the veins from closing. Or, we could open Levi's scalp and put in a muscle flap to protect the veins. We'd only want to do that surgery when he's older, though. It's not something you would elect to do unless it was absolutely necessary."

I noticed how, now, inserting a muscle flap or removing bones from Levi's head sounded like getting a cavity filled compared to the kinds of surgeries I'd feared. I was so relieved, I felt sick. I looked at Keith and saw that he was crying. I had only seen him cry twice before. Each time when his grandparent died.

Dr. Simon drew us a picture of a normal venous system and then one of what Levi's venous system looked like.

I asked, "If his veins start to close just on their own, what might you consider doing?"

"If Levi's veins were closing, we could do angioplasty or surgery. It is difficult to say because it all depends on what is occurring then."

I asked, "Can Levi live a normal life? Is his life expectancy normal?"

"Yes and yes. With sports, though—and this is crucial—he needs to wear protective gear. Always. While riding a bike, playing baseball he must always wear a helmet. We need the veins to stay open, and we don't want him to injure them in any way. You will need to be extra careful with him when he begins to crawl, too, especially on the stairs and around his brothers."

The outcome sunk in slowly: I got to go home with my baby, and the only problem I had to solve was protecting his fragile head. I thought of the other parents in that waiting room and how much they would give to have my outcome, my problem. We wrapped up our time with Dr. Simon by thanking him and shaking his hand. He told us a nurse would come take us to see Levi soon. Emerging back into the waiting room, it seemed slightly brighter, like a cloud had passed and let in the light.

Dear Sandy,

You have always been there for me. From installing fire alarms, to passing on Apple hand-me-downs, to sharing your passwords, to responding to my endless texts about ailments I have, and beyond. When I lived in Chicago and you came for business trips, you visited me, and we had adventures together. Our relationship grew, and I treasure those memories. I felt so important going with you on those fancy dinners with medical companies at all the greatest restaurants in town. I will always be especially grateful for the role you played in getting Levi to Boston. You were there every time I needed an email from a doctor deciphered. You helped me, so many times, to see the bigger picture and what the options were. If you told me I needed to take action, I listened. The stakes could not have been higher. I was getting more medical advice than any human could handle, and you bravely accepted my request to be my guide. You taught me to bring sweets for the nurses and to listen for the benefits versus the risks through all of the medical jargon. I have never trusted anyone while I was going through hell the way I trusted you. Your heart and care for humanity are admirable. I am proud to have you as my uncle. Your father would be so proud of the mensch you have become. I love you.

Chapter 43:

Best-Case Scenario

When we walked out of the consult room, although we were beyond excited, all the heavy looks on the faces of the parents put me in check. I looked at Keith. We exchanged a knowing look. In it was a shared understanding that we escaped a fatal bullet, and yet we had to rein in our relief and joy while we were on the waiting floor. Not every parent would be getting the kind of news we just received.

A few days later in Cleveland, the pediatric neurosurgeon from Boston, Dr. Thomas, called to explain the findings from his point of view. "The risks we see are with Levi's drainage. Because Levi's system drains through the scalp, it could be problematic if he ever has head trauma and bleeding. We don't want to go cutting any of those major veins because they're doing an important job." This was the reason the doctors were weary of that particular surgery. Dr. Thomas went on to explain that he didn't think Levi needed to wear a soft helmet during the toddling years on a day-to-day basis but definitely did during any sports. He explained if Levi did get a major cut or trauma in that area, it would bleed a lot. He actually said, "It will look like a Quentin Tarantino film."

He instructed us that if there was a bleed, we'd need to put firm pressure on the veins and then call 911 immediately.

"Once Levi begins walking, and, therefore, standing upright, the visibility of the veins should diminish, since the blood will flow down through the neck due to gravity. Levi has an unusual variant of an abnormal vein, which again, no one has ever seen before."

Dr. Thomas was the most qualified pediatric neurosurgeon in the country and would be responsible for any surgeries in the future. He had an ease about him, and I enjoyed listening to him. When I asked questions about the future, he said, "It's hard to say because we've never seen this before. A slow closure of the venous system is almost always completely tolerated because the system will build alternative routes over time. If there were any major changes that happened too quickly though, we would need to do another angiogram."

"So you wouldn't do a surgery even in that case?"

"I would only consider doing a surgery to treat the actual veins. Even then, I would only, and I mean *only*, do the surgery if I was backed up against a wall and the wall was on fire. But because this is likely from a clot that happened before birth, I don't think it will be a progressive problem. My two main concerns are trauma and clotting."

"And what about how the veins have grown bigger and more prominent over the past month or so?"

"It could be because there is a great deal of brain growth at this age."

We thanked him and got off the phone. I turned to Keith expectantly, wanting to talk everything over and process all our feelings, but he just gave me a tight smile and walked out of the room.

When I first became a mom, I stared at Franklin and felt so much fear about how fast time was passing. With each son, that fear grew. I was worried that I would miss them as little babies, and I wished I could slow it all down, savor it more. That grief that comes with each rapid stage in a child's first five years, the loss of that previous version of your child, though buffered by the gain of the new version, it became the biggest fear in my life.

And then came Levi and everything that led up to Boston. With each picture I took, I wondered, *Will this be the last picture I take of him?* But now, suddenly, that big, bad fear was gone. I was no longer afraid that my boys would grow too fast. Now, I was terrified they would be frozen in time. Frozen in a picture, never to be older than they were in that captured moment. In the midst of all we went through with Levi, this was a massive gift.

I now wanted my children to grow. I wanted them to go to kindergarten and graduate third grade. I thought about the day I would, hopefully, drop my sons off at college, and I treasured the idea of even their absence in my house if it meant they were out there in the world, alive. Three of my favorite people have that frozen picture in place of their living children growing up too fast. This perspective was a gift that changed everything. The choice to be grateful for life in each moment became my freedom. I get to celebrate the milestones. I get to watch them grow up.

Chapter 44:

The Other Shoe

The summer after Boston was filled with trips taking Levi back and forth to Dr. Joseph's office with fevers and ear infections. No big deal. Levi, like his older brothers, would need ear tubes. This, I could handle. As the fevers continued, though, and antibiotics failed to clear the infections, I worried. I knew something was wrong. My other boys always responded to antibiotics. Something was off. I could feel it.

Levi was always warm. I took his temperature daily. He was having daily fevers. Nothing too high, but I'd never seen a kid with a daily fever of 100–101 with no apparent cause. People asked me about my thermometers. They didn't believe me, even when I took my own temperature or the other boys' temperatures, which were normal and Levi's still was not. I bought different kinds of thermometers. I even resorted to using a baby rectal thermometer. All of the temperature readings were the same. I kept a log of his fevers.

By August, I went to see Dr. Joseph. I had the feeling everyone around me thought I was crazy or that I had Munchausen by proxy. But Dr. Joseph agreed that it was puzzling, especially with Levi's failure to respond to the multiple antibiotic shots they had given him. Dr. Joseph recommended we take a trip to see Dr. T. Dr. T was an allergy and immunology doctor, who I had visited once before when we thought Elijah had an allergy to milk.

Levi screamed and cried the day I took him in. He had diarrhea and an ugly, raised chin rash. Dr. T's face lit up when I mentioned two clues. First, Levi didn't start showing any sign of health issues until he was six months old. Second, he didn't respond to the intensely strong antibiotic shots. Dr. T ordered blood tests.

Here we were again. I knew it. I knew we were not done. I could feel the impending doom of the journey we were about to embark on to discover the unknown medical mystery. But I also knew that if I could walk through Boston, I could handle whatever was next. Boston was my acid test for life. I had not escaped unscathed, but I welcomed my battle scars over the alternative any day.

A few days later, we were back in Dr. T's office discussing the results of the bloodwork. I didn't bring Levi's medical journal to write down what he was saying because I'd naïvely hoped there would be nothing to write. Dr. T told me that Levi was deficient in IgA, or immunoglobulin A, which is an antibody that plays a crucial role in the immune function of mucous membranes. It helps defend the body from airborne illnesses. More than deficient, Levi had none. Not even low numbers. He had absolutely no IgA.

I imagined a football field with a quarterback and no offensive linemen. If someone was sick and coughed on or touched him, there was a high chance Levi would catch whatever they had. He had no protection. I looked down at him. He had thrown himself on the floor, and was crying, and snotty, laying on the floor. The dirty, disease-covered floor of a doctor's office. Purell. I needed Purell.

Because Levi's numbers were normal in the other two parts of the immune system, it was very likely that he would never grow IgA. And he couldn't receive any blood products with IgA in them because there could be a fatal reaction in his blood. I thought, *Holy shit.* He dodged a massive bullet in Boston. They would have given him blood filled with IgA. No one would have known why he was having a bad reaction. They would have assumed it was his venous anomaly.

Dr. T wasn't done. "We need to do more tests. I don't like some of his other lab numbers. I want to do a test to see how Levi responds to a vaccination. Then more blood work."

I asked a familiar question: "What are you looking for?"

"Let's not get ahead of ourselves. It's a little premature to worry."

"I'm the kind of person that needs to know what's going on, and I need you to tell me what you are concerned about."

He sighed. "If Levi's numbers stay low in response to this vaccination, that would be really bad. That could mean that he has a defect in his immune system that could lead to medical terminology no parent wants to talk about." As it was, having IgA deficiency was no amusement park, but it was not too uncommon. Dr. T said we would need to wait three weeks to find out if Levi had an additional functional defect.

Even though I often told friends and family to never go online after leaving a doctor's office, I couldn't always follow that advice. I wanted to know everything. The only problem is, Google doesn't filter their information based on who is searching. There was too much information. I saw horrible scenarios, cancers, and mortality rates. "Malignant" came up under symptoms. I got that burning sensation in my stomach and chest.

When we went to Dr. T's office for the results, I was cautiously optimistic, but inside, I expected the worst. I had devoured all the information about it online and didn't see any of the telling signs in Levi. Luckily, I was right. He did not have this scary immune defect. He just had IgA deficiency and the venous anomaly we already knew about.

Chapter 45:

PTSD

That winter was an ugly one. I missed my dog, Ruby, who I had to give away the previous winter during all that led to Boston. I had a completely undiagnosed case of PTSD. I lacked the desire and energy to seek out help, and I was living my life like every day was war. Levi's fevers were getting higher. In December, he had a temperature of 105.

I had never seen a fever so high. I called the after-hours number for Dr. T's office, and the nurse on call advised, "Go to the ER immediately." The problem was, because of his IgA deficiency, the ER was the last place the doctors wanted us to go. It was a breeding ground for infection. But 105 was too high to stay home, and the nurse was concerned about a dangerous infection he may have already had.

Levi was floppy and red. I raced downtown to Rainbow Emergency Room. Keith stayed home with the other two boys. I forgot to bring Levi's shoes. I was explaining all his medical conditions to the doctors, and they were staring at me in disbelief. We needed three adults to hold him down to get the IV in to take more blood. He was sick of being poked. Hours later, we found out he had a respiratory infection.

A few weeks later, he spiked another high fever: 104 one day then 105 the next. The first handful of times, I took him to the ER, but each subsequent time there was no explanation for the fever. No infection, no virus. He was suffering, and no one knew what was going on. Dr. T said, "Levi isn't displaying symptoms of a typical IgA deficiency."

As time went on, the fevers came every few days at the most to once a week at the least. Though it became the routine, it never felt normal. I was afraid and on fire with worry. I contacted the doctors in Boston to ask if the two medical conditions could possibly be related. The answer was that it was unlikely, but they couldn't know for sure. How could one person have two completely rare medical issues that weren't connected? But no one knew, no one was answering any questions, and without any changes in the high fevers and their regularity, years passed.

During that time, we went to specialist after specialist. We saw seven in Cleveland alone: rheumatologists, geneticists, gastrointestinal (GI) doctors, immunologists, and on, and on. We tried different medications. There were endless tests and blood draws. Levi's blood was drawn a minimum of four times a week. During one of his annual MRIs, a GI specialist took advantage of that period of sedation and did an exhaustive search of his GI system. Also piggybacking on this sedation was a second MRI of his chest because by that time, when Levi was three, the bulging blue veins had spread from his head to snake across his pectus-shaped chest, as well. Doctors wanted to rule out any problems with the blood flow in and out of his heart.

Perhaps it was because of the extra length of the sedation. Maybe it was a new kind of anesthesia. Whatever the reason, Levi didn't wake up normally from the anesthesia. He screamed and flailed. He flapped, and kicked, and wailed, and was inconsolable for almost an hour. I had no idea how physically strong he was. I couldn't hold him or calm him down. The nurses told us Levi was having a bad reaction to the anesthesia. He was having more than a bad reaction. He was not the same child.

While we waited to consult with the GI specialist after the tests, I felt sorry for myself. I worried I wouldn't be able to go on like this if they didn't figure out what was wrong with him soon and be able to treat it. While I was feeling that way, I saw a man and his son sitting across the room. The boy, older than Levi, was paralyzed from the neck down. His father was so gentle with him. He spoke softly to him. They appeared to be regulars at the hospital. I heard the man tell the nurse that his son was only able to digest baby formula. It was all I needed to shift my perspective and realize I had it easy. I watched the man pick up his son like a baby, and the boy's head hung back, and he looked at his father with such love and humility. They were a gift. I could do this.

The GI specialist said, "I have no clear medical reason for what is causing Levi's problems. I think you will need to seek out another specialist." And so I did. And then another and another. Each specialist did their workup, and when they could not find an answer, they sent us to someone else. When Levi was almost five, one doctor actually said, "Mom, what you need to do is stop taking his temperature and send him to school." Some of them didn't even believe me. They didn't believe his fevers could reach such high temperatures. But they did. And as I watched the number on the dreaded thermometer climb, and laid my hands on my son's fiery skin, I felt that burning heat inside my own body rise up to answer.

Chapter 46:

God Is Crying, Too

After twelve years of sobriety and five years of fevers and scary veins and unanswered questions about my son, my doubt in God had grown. My struggle was a quiet one. Only those who really knew me caught the subtle changes in my reactions to comments like, "Everything happens for a reason." And to my all-time least favorite, "This is God's will." I hated hearing well-meaning people say it was impossible to have faith and fear in the same moment.

Dark, angry, honest Carly came out. What I wanted to say was, "Bullshit!" I wanted to see what their faith looked like when it was their baby's life at stake. I wanted them to explain in those moments how hearing that *everything happens for a reason* would make them feel. Were they comforted by that idea when their back was up against the wall? When it really counted? When the outcome was unclear and no one could tell me that everything would be okay?

I went to see a therapist I'd seen when I was younger. His name was Jake Chapman, and he went by Chapman, which I liked. He had a serious face with hard angles and soft eyes. When I was younger, he was the one therapist in a long line of them who came closest to making a difference for me. Because he said it straight and in ways that made sense. When I went back to him all those years later, he said, "You're like a soldier who has come back from war. You're still in your fatigues with your weapon in hand, ready to shoot. But the war is over, and you don't know how to put the weapon down." But to me, the war didn't feel like it was over.

I dove into the sober textbook that I have trusted with my life and searched for an answer. I had to find a God that would work for me, because the one I had so cherished and revered for the past eleven years no longer did. I was looking for a statement or suggestion which would tell me that to have a relationship with God, I would have to trust that everything that happened in life was part of God's plan. If I found that statement, I didn't know where I would be able to go.

To my great relief, I failed to find that line. What I did find was that I needed to have a God of my own conception. That if I stuck close to that God and performed that God's work to the best of my ability, I would be given all I needed to handle whatever life threw at me. That, I could live with. I no longer believed that God had a plan for me and that every little piece of my life was laid out in detail. I no longer believed that everything happened for a reason. Now, I believed in a God that would give me all the support, love, strength, courage, and guidance I needed to get through each day.

I remembered a story from one of my favorite women in recovery, Ro. She told about how she imagined God. "There was a young boy, around ten years old, in the Pediatric ICU with burns all over his body. He couldn't be turned or settled in a way that didn't make him scream in pain. Two nurses stood by his door and one whispered to the other, 'Where is God now?' The other nurse whispered back, 'God is sitting by that boy's bed, crying with him.'"

It was a story that allowed God to be love and presence rather than a target for blame when anything hard or painful happens. It made room for horrors to happen, like abuse, and slavery, and the Holocaust, and sick children, and God's intervention was comfort and presence in each moment. It was subtle yet powerful. The design of this world includes cause and effect, agency and will, and other neutral, objective laws that everyone must live with. God could be a guide and a support through that unpredictable, unsafe forest. This was a God I could believe in.

What helped me most was thinking of God's role in my life as that of a loving parent. A great parent would do anything to shield their child from harm but is not able to prevent life from happening. I saw God as my parent. God sat by me and comforted me while I cried. And like a great parent, God wept with me when life was seemingly unbearable. This became my new truth. It was backed by evidence in my own life that I could not refute. I have always been given what I need to walk through life. It hasn't always been fun or the way I would have wanted it, but when I look back, I can see and feel the support. It reminded me of a Hemingway line: "The world breaks everyone and afterward many are strong in the broken places." I felt strong in the places where life had broken me.

Although this new conception of God made sense to me, it seemed to insult and disturb many people around me. Including my own mother and many people in recovery. I was no longer able to nod and agree when those statements about everything being God's will were offered to someone in pain. I never felt the need to stand at a podium and tell them they were wrong, but I did feel an obligation to share my experience with people who were suffering. I did it quietly and, mostly, with tact. But I was still angry, and it wasn't at

God. I was angry at the idea that what had comforted me for so long was bullshit to me now.

Life would happen, and a like a great parent, God could not stop life from happening. But God could love me while it happened.

Chapter 47:

Misdiagnosed

While I waited for the genetic tests to come back, I realized that I fully expected them to all be negative. I'd grown so used to these diagnostic tests revealing nothing. I was resigned to the constant searching. Why did his temperature start out normal when he woke up and within thirty minutes, rise to 100–100.5 degrees? What was going on inside of my son? He was cranky and uncomfortable. When Keith would say, "Sometimes kids are just cranky," I felt unheard. I wished he would spend a whole day or week with Levi and see what I saw. I wished he could see it, and question, and wonder, and worry like I did. When my own husband thought I was crazy and making things up, I knew I was completely alone.

If I wasn't crazy and there really was something wrong, what did that mean for Levi? Would more be revealed? Would there be treatments, more specialists, and more doctor visits? Would his condition improve or worsen? What would the quality of his life be? What about mine? Or Franklin and Elijah's? Would Keith find acceptance and patience with Levi?

My chest always felt weighted and constricted. I was overwhelmed and afraid. I was uncertain about my next move at every turn. Chapman became my guiding voice. He asked me to write at the top of each page in my journal: *What if I'm not crazy?* I spent three pages not writing about it and then finally, *What if I'm not imagining all this? What then? What does that mean for Levi? For me? For our family? If I'm not imagining all this, then something really is wrong with my baby. Something beyond his neurovascular system being so rare that there are no other known cases.*

If Levi's immune system isn't doing its job, what about school? Would he ever be able to go? I knew he would, but would I need to have a totally different expectation of his attendance? *Will I ever be able to have a regular job? Who would pick up the calls from the nurse?*

The questioning and worrying was all about fear and feeling alone. Keith didn't go to the specialist appointments with us. He didn't experience what I dealt with on a daily basis. I was the only one invested in the charting, questioning, and even worrying. It was his apathy that made me feel crazy in comparison. I projected it on to everyone else, believing everyone doubted my validity. All I could do was trust myself and keep searching.

When Levi was five, a routine blood test came back to reveal that Levi was no longer IgA deficient. It was low, but low in the normal range. Around the same time, his daily fevers stopped. They came less frequently, about once every few weeks. I started to see a pattern in his fevers, though they were, by no means, in a consistent rhythm. He would spike a 105- or 106-degree fever, and I would take him to the ER or doctor, where they would not be able to find an infection or source of the fever, and we'd leave without a plan or an answer. I'd just give him fever-reducing medications around the clock until the fever passed. He'd get inflamed rashes on his chin, painful sores in his mouth, and awful GI pain, but no one could figure out why. I treated the symptoms and continued knowing nothing.

Steroids worked like deploying a special ops team to handle a house intruder whom they sprayed with bullets from automatic assault rifles. They completely wiped out the fevers, but they also made him crazy. Screaming and kicking crazy. Apparently, this was a rare reaction that some people have to steroids.

Dr. T and Dr. Joseph agreed it was likely some type of autoinflammatory disorder, but couldn't confirm which one. There was no formal diagnosis Levi's symptoms were totally consistent with. That is how he ended up as a subject of research at the National Institutes of Health (NIH).

First, Levi's doctors sent his chart to a research group in Europe that took on rare and unique medical cases to solve. That group declined to study Levi because they took on only cases they were confident they could successfully treat and, therefore, solve. Next they sent his chart to the NIH. Months later, I received a call from them asking us to visit a pediatric research hospital in Bethesda, Maryland called The Children's Inn.

Meanwhile, Keith and I were building and preparing to move in to our dream home. My parents gave us a piece of property behind their house, and we rented an apartment while we built the exact home we wanted on that lot. With all the tension still between us and the chaos of constructing and moving into a new home, I didn't feel excited about the NIH. I worried it was a waste of time because not even the best doctors and most respected specialists in the country were able to figure anything out about Levi. And he'd been doing better in those most recent months. He was having fewer and less severe fevers.

Instead of feeling excited, I talked about the NIH as if it were a dreaded obligation. Secretly, I was afraid it would be more doctors telling us they didn't know what was wrong or what to do. Also, I was afraid of looking like an imposter. What if the doctors looked at Levi and didn't see anything wrong with him and asked us why were we wasting their time? Keith didn't offer to join us, so my mom made arrangements to come along so I didn't have to be alone.

All the transitions were getting Elijah really worked up, and he was having behavioral problems. I begged my mom to not come with us to NIH and stay home with the boys. I told her that it wasn't a big deal and that I could handle this. I didn't want her to be bored with all the waiting and testing. I didn't want to burden her. I hated accepting help.

As the visit date quickly approached, my anxiety grew. I tried to convince myself to cancel it because Levi was seemingly doing better. I even asked Dr. Joseph for his permission to cancel, and he jokingly told me he would punch me out if I did. He knew the time would come when Levi would get sick again and we would continue to have no explanation. It's funny how the mind works so fiercely to deny the truth to protect itself from what causes pain. But in so doing, the mind is deceitful and damaging.

One day while my boys were at camp, the number to the camp popped up on my phone. I felt my nerves spike, like when a dog sees another animal across the street and its hackles go up. The voice of a teenager came over the phone, "Levi had a little accident," and my heart dropped deep into my belly and caught on fire. I considered so much in those milliseconds. My mind raced ahead into action: *Which hospital to race to and who to call. I'd call my mom to pick up the other boys. I'd call Boston. Should I call Boston right now or wait to see what the ER docs say?* And then I heard my own voice asking, "Where did Levi have the accident?"

"At the pool,"

"No, where on his body?"

"No, no! He is fine. He had a little accident in his bathing suit."

I exhaled for the first time since I picked up her call. I explained that he is on medicine that makes his belly sick. Just like that, cool, calm, and collected Carly was back.

"Throw him in the shower and toss away his bathing suit. He's the third kid to wear those trunks. I do not want those back."

Dear Dr. T,

> You have followed Levi's case since he was nine months old, when he couldn't get rid of all those infections and had to have insane amounts of bloodwork. You are the doctor who eventually told us we needed more help and contacted the group in Europe and then the NIH. You are the doctor I learned to ask, "If this was your kid, what would you do?" And I would watch you picture one of your three sons. You would answer not only as a physician but as a parent. All these years later, as we listened to nine-year-old (or 109-year-old?) Levi tell us how he knew when he was about to get sick before the thermometer knew. Telling us how he manages bloodwork and shots. How he breathes to calm himself. Telling us how to live in a sometimes

inhospitable body as though he's been doing it for a century already. And then you tell us that Levi shouldn't have to live like this. That this isn't the quality of life you want for him, because you have seen him tear it up on the soccer field. You know this is not a kid who wants to be sick every month. You remind me that none of us really know what's wrong with Levi and that anyone who thinks they definitively know what's wrong and what to do doesn't know what they're talking about. Thank you for the reminder to pace myself during the overwhelming times. This medical journey is also Levi's life. Where once I needed to know what was wrong and what to do, now I just need to take care of my son and be grateful and kind. Thank you for reminding me that we don't have to do this, we *get* to do this.

Chapter 48:

The NIH

Right before I left, I talked with my closest friends and was reminded that I could do this. Even though it was demanding and overwhelming, I had the tools. I was also reminded that I'm not alone. I was hurt that Keith wasn't coming with us. I reasoned that maybe he was scared and in denial. The morning we left was full of tension. Levi was sick. He was extra clingy, cranky, and sleepy. I was nervous; my stomach killed, and my eye twitched. As I was running around the house packing last minute items, I mentioned to Keith that I was embarrassed that he was not showing up for something so important. We got in a fight, and he finally understood how big of a deal it was. But I didn't have time to deal with him trying to work out whether to get to Bethesda. I needed to have my head focused on Levi and be mentally prepared for a new medical journey. Keith decided later that he would fly to meet us there, but it felt too late. I just needed to take care of Levi.

Levi had a team of specialists assigned to him whose job it was to look for questions that no one else had asked. I had very little hope of anything coming from the visit and felt like a bit of a fraud when I looked around at some of the patients there who seemed to have truly dire medical problems. I worried we stole someone's seat. We stayed right next to the hospital at The Children's Inn. Our stay was completely paid for, and it was wonderful. I was relieved that my mom didn't listen to me and came along. There was no way I could have answered hours and hours of questions while Levi whined and wanted to leave.

After only two days (that felt like two weeks), I still hadn't shaken the feeling that we didn't belong. The campus was completely fenced off by strict security. The doctors were extremely intelligent. I worried Levi wasn't sick enough. Then I realized that maybe I was too afraid to deal with the reality that he actually was qualified to be there.

The other patients at the NIH had illnesses all over the spectrum, and doctors discovered diagnoses for only about one-third of them. I tried to imagine what it would feel like if they said, "This is it. This is what your son has." It might not be such a great diagnosis to receive. But would it bring relief to at least know?

I forced myself to absolutely reject the notion that some others had planted in my head over the years: That nothing was even wrong with Levi and I was just a paranoid mother. That notion wasn't mine. It came from other people. And although they were sometimes well-meant, they had been wrong. I always knew there was something wrong. We all knew there was something wrong. As a parent, I felt so powerless. And that powerlessness made me want to believe the well-meaning doubters. It made me want to downplay his painful illnesses and high fevers and focus on the times he seemed to be a healthy, normal boy.

I asked the doctor if we should resign ourselves to life the way it was: Levi seems totally healthy at times, and also gets extremely sick with very high fevers at times. "No," she said, "that's not sufficient." I needed to hear those words. Levi belonged there.

The team started Levi on a new medication that would end up helping with his mouth sores, slightly lowering his fevers, and giving him chronic GI issues. We were not free, but I was willing to take it. I could breathe. I even tried to ignore other well-meaning people like friends and people in meetings telling me everything would work out the way it was supposed to. I didn't believe that, but I was so thankful for our fortune. We were not done, but at least we were not talking about testing for sibling matches or finding bone marrow samples.

After we returned home, Levi spiked a fever again. More ear infections, and sores, and fevers with intervals of apparent health and wellness ensued. For a few months, it seemed life was slipping back to normalcy. Although there were still intermittent fevers and infections, the medicine from the NIH seemed to help. Keith said, "I think we are finally done with Levi's immune problems." But I didn't feel as confident.

Things took a turn when a 105-degree fever took us to the ER. The ER doctors didn't know Levi and didn't believe me when I told them his history. They didn't seem to have access to his record and acted like they'd never heard of an autoinflammatory condition before. They couldn't locate a source of infection, so they sent us home. They told us to continue giving Levi fever-reducing medicine and keep an eye on him. We went back home where I gave Levi Tylenol and set the alarm to wake him in three hours to give him Advil. The same old drill from most ER doctors we'd seen. At 5:00 a.m., I heard Levi moaning. I leapt out of bed and found him lethargic and flushed. His body was hot to the touch. His cheeks were bright red, and the thermometer read 107.4. I had never seen a fever go so high. I called the NIH's emergency number, and the doctor who answered said, "Go to the ER immediately."

We went back. And we went back again. And again. Dr. Joseph explained that once a fever hits 108 degrees, the protein in the body begins to break down, which can cause permanent brain and muscle damage. The scary high fevers kept coming. With each fever over 107, I raced to the ER, where they did more blood work and testing. It was exhausting and frightening for both Levi and me, and it did not stop. My other two boys barely saw me, and tension between Keith and I grew thicker by the day. I walked the balance beam, and I hesitated to take the next step. And I felt God's strong hand and heard God's clear voice. "I've got you." And I took another slow and careful step and felt terrified and looked back. And I felt God's hand and I heard God's voice. "I've got you."

Three weeks into the almost daily high fevers, we had another seven-hour visit to the ER. The same story followed, as there was no apparent cause for the fever. Levi's inflammation numbers were staggering, and the ER doctors gave him IV antibiotics just empirically. They couldn't believe a fever could recur and be so high unless there was some infection somewhere. We left with discharge papers that told us to immediately go back to the ER if Levi's fever reached 106. Levi spiked a 107 a few hours after we got home.

When the ER doctor asked Levi what he had for dinner the night before, he answered, "Cereal because my mom was sad." True, but I was also stressed out and terrified. We were living in the unknown again, trying to stay present while people in the world around us were dealing with tragedies of their own.

I sat in an ER waiting room watching the news coverage from the Connecticut shootings at Newtown Elementary School. I cried as I watched the faces of parents who will never hold their children again. I was holding my boy. He may have been burning up, and he may have had more challenges ahead of him, but he had a chance. He was alive.

I learned to keep my mouth closed when someone around me experienced a life-changing loss. I could only hurt as I thought of their circumstances and let it make me appreciative of my own. When I saw a beautiful sky, I would point it out to my sons. I thought of all the parents I'd met along the way who no longer could. Sometimes, I let the despair just press me into the moment, and I found deep gratitude there. I would hold my boys close to my chest and thank life for that one moment.

When I took Levi to the NIH for the second time, they took more blood, and ran more tests, and studied my charts and logs of all his fevers and symptoms. They kept watch over him and monitored the patterns of his fevers for days. Then, they prescribed a new injection for me to give him in addition to the weekly injection. When Levi spiked a high fever it would stop the inflammation and bring the fever down within a few hours. The only downfall was that the injection was incredibly painful for Levi. He feared it terribly, and screamed, and cried, and had to be physically restrained to receive it.

There was still no diagnosis. He was still our unicorn. But they were making progress on his treatments, anyway. This gave me a hope I hadn't felt in years.

Chapter 49:

Fault Lines

I don't know exactly when it started, but I found myself editing how I spoke around Keith to avoid having more silent fights. I kept all my true feelings from him. We were only intimate on his schedule, and when I tried to talk to him about it, he would tell me that my sex drive was abnormal. Although I'd tried several different ways over the years to communicate how much that wasn't working for me, it never seemed to click, or maybe I wasn't being clear. It seemed like he had zero attraction to me. It was the loneliest I'd ever felt inside of a relationship. I would walk by him in only my panties and it was as if I was invisible. Whenever we talked about it, I ended up feeling like something was wrong with me. I wondered if as he had gotten to know me more, he realized he didn't really want to be with the real me.

One Friday night, I told him I was considering leaving. He was so calm receiving the news. He didn't say anything except to ask if he could go watch a basketball game. Over the weekend, it was crickets. There didn't even seem to be tension anymore. It was all replaced by an ocean of silence. One would think after your wife tells you she's thinking of leaving that you'd have further things to say or ask. But he was quieter than ever. I realized then that I'd been hoping my threat would wake him up and make him tune into the relationship.

Our problems were not singular. There were so many things that went into the ever-widening break between us. My marriage did not survive having a child with potentially fatal medical conditions, but it did not crumble because of it. Levi was not and will never be responsible for what happened between his father and me. What I learned about marriage is that it is a living, breathing organism that can only thrive if tended to by both parties. It is the one school project that cannot win an award if only one member of the team does the work. It will only continue to beat and breathe if both lovers are willing to put 100 percent of their heart, soul, sweat, and vulnerability into it.

Looking back, I saw through the clarity of hindsight that my marriage had deep cracks before there were ever children. We had very different ideas about a handful of personal values that we would not discover until life presented them to us. There was no betrayal, but there was neglect. The loneliness that lived in our master suite was smothering, but whenever I brought it up, we could not discuss it for too long. He wanted to blame me, and I wanted to blame him. Looking back, I see a tableau of the two of us sitting on the edge of the bed in our custom-designed master suite, inside our dream home that we built together, scowling and pointing fingers at one another.

Part Three:
The Fire

Chapter 50:

Dream Home

I have lived in my actual dream house. I designed it from visions in my mind. I contributed to the blueprints, used my own hands in the building of the foundation, and chose every color, tile, finish, and vintage light fixture. I believe that beautiful house kept my marriage together for a time because our strength as a couple was one that could only be exploited in that project—we really enjoyed antiquing, and we have very similar architectural tastes. It became this physical structure that held us together through that time. It was built on land that my parents gifted us, and the inside was adorned with wallpaper flown in from England, a fire mantle from the turn of the century, exquisite crown molding, and crystal chandeliers. But even all that beauty couldn't keep our marriage from falling apart. To start, we couldn't afford to live there. No matter how much we cut back, we couldn't make it work. But the bigger problem was that although the house itself was our dream, the home we created inside of it wasn't.

For a while, I thought it was the money. I offered the idea to sell our dream house, which would allow Keith to quit the job he despised, and we could buy a small home within our means and have less stress and more time together. But he didn't want to live in a small house, and for him, the time spent at the job he loathed was worth it for the money he would one day make.

I asked, "What is the number that would justify the loss of our marriage?" But he couldn't hear me. We had been to couple's therapy on and off for years, and it was the same conversation: I was unhappy, and he was just fine.

No matter how much I exercised or what I did to my body to be attractive, it was as if I was invisible. I was a woman walking around a man who couldn't see me or hear me. Regardless of how confident and strong I had become, not feeling wanted by the only man who was supposed to desire me made me feel lonely, even while lying next to him. I did everything I could to invite him into the dance of growth and change that could help us reconnect, but it was as though I had no one to dance with. No matter how I asked or how many times I repeated it, he couldn't hear me. He wouldn't begin to fight for us until I had finally given up.

On the night I finally gave up, we set the boys up to watch a show and talked. We sat on opposite sides of our king-sized bed, staring away from each other. He brought up how I always wanted him to be more than who he was: more open, more connected, more physical, more romantic, and more communicative. But this time when he brought it up, it didn't seem like my request was such a crime. This time, it seemed like a reasonable request from a spouse to their beloved. I agreed that I did want more, and it seemed that he wanted less.

He wanted me to be less needy, less physical, less communicative, less demanding, less inappropriate. I wanted more Keith, and he wanted less Carly. When I said those words out loud and he agreed, I felt the end roll down my cheeks with the tears. I had worked so hard to get to a place where I not only felt like I was good enough, but where I loved the woman I had become. And now, I had to face the house-shattering truth that I was in a marriage where my husband didn't want to choose the woman I had worked so hard to choose.

Once I understand a truth within myself, I can't pretend like I don't know it. I couldn't live holding a grenade after the pin had been pulled, smiling and acting like everything was great. Sharp pains in my belly and constant nausea plagued me. I worried that because of my previous suicide attempt and history of countless psych meds, people took me less seriously when I said I was struggling or unhappy. People tended to chalk it up to a propensity for drama on my part. This made me doubt the validity of my own feelings and question what I knew was true deep inside.

Levi's medical situation was also a distraction from the problems in our marriage, putting any action about it on a permanent hold. Between the marital unrest and the progression of Levi's unexplained illness, I struggled silently. There was not enough concealer in the world to hide the dark circles under my eyes.

Chapter 51:

Mitchell's Journey

Despite Levi's usual sunny disposition in preschool (minus the time he told the entire class Santa Claus wasn't real), he sometimes struggled with his energy levels and came home red-cheeked and floppy. That usually meant a flare-up was soon to follow. During our first visit to the NIH, the original team of doctors considered attributing his undiagnosed condition to just being young and in preschool. The doctors put him on medications that made him slightly better but still not well. By the end of February, I had been in the ER with him four times in six weeks. He couldn't get healthy, and I was finally losing hope.

I hadn't yet succumbed to self-pity about Levi's condition. I had always looked to kids worse off to help shift my perspective toward gratitude. But this was rough. I was almost exclusively caring for Levi as my mom took care of my other boys. The guilt of being pulled away from Franklin and Elijah was taxing. I was in a dark place and couldn't find gratitude.

It was March 2, 2013. I was scrolling through Facebook on my phone while waiting in the car outside of Starbucks in Chagrin Falls when I saw a post that changed my life. I had never heard of Mitchell before that day and would never forget him after. Someone shared a post by a man named Chris Jones, who was Mitchell's father. Chris posted that Mitchell died earlier that day. I read, and wept, and spent the entire day reading every post related to Mitchell's Journey. I scrolled all the way down to the beginning when Mitchell was three, and Chris first began posting about Mitchell's story.

I read post after post, witnessing a journey that had touched and altered so many lives. The cascade was like a widening river system, with water branching and branching into hundreds then thousands of rivulets, nourishing far and wide. I could not stop crying. Not only was the story intense, but Chris was a remarkable writer. He had a way of expressing words and emotions with a tenderness and openness I hadn't seen in many other fathers. Between my own father and Keith, I did not have a lot of male examples expressing this kind of raw, open emotion. I was mesmerized.

I began reading and sharing Chris' posts daily as I watched his grief unfurl. It became a spiritual experience for me— one where I was internally transformed in the way I see, feel, experience, and live my life. Stumbling upon Mitchell's Journey gave me one of the greatest gifts of my entire life: perspective. And ultimately, it would give me the greatest gift of my life: my soul mate. Though I knew none of this at the time.

The ER visits with Levi continued, but I coped with them differently. As I sat with Levi's fevered little body in my lap and interacted with ER doctors who had no clue how to proceed, I never again felt sorry for myself. Instead, I searched the posts on Mitchell's page for the next bit of inspiration. I'd think, *Mitchell's parents, Chris and Natalie, would kill to have Mitchell, sick, alive, on their chest right now.* My perspective had been transformed.

Fast forward to October. I read Christopher's posts daily. I was hungry for gratitude. My heart broke for the parents out there who had it so much worse. I was thankful for my child's illnesses. I drafted an email to Chris in my head for weeks before I sent it. Why would I send it? He had over 250,000 followers. He would never even read it. But my letter wasn't about him reading it. It was about me writing it. Telling him with my inadequate words how his powerful story changed my life. Sharing a piece of my struggles and my heart. I sent it on October 4th, 2013 and never gave it another thought.

Chris,

I have been writing to you in my head since last March. I didn't know about Mitchell's Journey until right at his end. I am a woman who is a spiritual warrior and a seeker. Last March, I was weakened by my own circumstances with my youngest son, Levi. It was the first time in our medical journey that I felt lost and hopeless and when I found your story. I found my God's strength, and my purpose was reignited.

I'm sure you know that one of the gifts that God has given you is the ability to speak to others through your words. I bet you have had this gift your whole life. I bet you had no idea when your personal hell began that it would change the lives of so many around the world.

I know this does nothing to ease your pain. I am writing you to simply say, "Thank you," and let you know that not one day goes by that Mitchell and your family are not in my thoughts, and they are being used to buoy my spirits.

I have sat in the ER holding my baby, searching for your latest post to give me strength and gratitude. I have told those around me that you would give anything for the opportunity to sit in another ER with your son on your chest. Because of your willingness to share your heart and life with us, I am able to continue.

I do not know what the future holds for Levi. He has two extremely rare and potentially life-threatening conditions that puzzle the brightest doctors in the country. He is the unicorn in their examination rooms.

Levi has completely altered my perception of God, life, people, and understanding. He causes me more pain and more joy than anyone I know. He is my Mitchell, and I look to you for guidance.

You could have easily chosen to keep this journey private. You could have, understandably, kept your pain and your experience close to your heart. But because you made the decision to reach out and share, my journey is one with purpose and direction, and I know that no matter what comes down the road, I will continue to walk because you are.

Sending love and gratitude to you and your beautiful family,

Carly

I continued reading his posts and searching for gratitude as I advocated for my son and felt the loneliness of my imperfect marriage.

Dear Isaac,

You are one of the people who changed the way I define love and how I prioritize my life. When you speak, I am able to hear every word you say. The first time I heard you speak, I was barely able to keep up with my notes because everything you said was like truth serum to me. The second time I heard you speak was at a *Shabbaton*, and because it was Shabbos, I was not allowed to write down anything you said. So I leaned in and did my best to focus and listen. The topic was love. You illuminated a topic I thought I had understood but realized I was clueless about. You said that real love is when you want to know more about the person you love. When you want to see them and for them to see you. To hear them and for them to hear you. I wanted that so intensely. I cried after that talk because I did not have that in my marriage. When I brought it up to my husband, it was met with confusion and nervous laughter. I felt something shift within me and knew that you had revealed a truth that made me uncomfortable but that had also awakened me. Thank you for teaching me to first identify the five most important things to me and then to take a look at my life and see if I am spending my time on those five things. Prioritizing the things that matter in order of importance makes me so uncomfortable. But then again, people who open my mind the most usually make me the most uncomfortable. I will never forget how intensely I felt about what you said and how much light you brought to my world. I am forever appreciative of you.

My top five—in order—because it matters:

1. My relationship with God and my sobriety
2. My family
3. My relationship with myself
4. Being a light in the world around me
5. Living a life that matters

Chapter 52:

Emotionally Hungry

Despite the shattering realization of Keith wanting less Carly and me wanting more Keith, I kept trying to make my marriage work. I reached out to Keith over and over. I talked about the problems between us for years. We had six years of therapy, marriage counselors, and clear direct talks with tears in my eyes under our belts. I begged him to see how wide the chasm between us was getting. I wanted so badly to connect. After everything that happened with Levi in Boston, compounded by his fevers and new medical scares, I fundamentally changed as a mother, a wife, and a human.

We sat in front of our therapist, Chapman, and I told Keith, "Here's the thing: this journey with Levi has shown me that life is precious, and we need to live it now. I need you to know that your lack of support and strength has made things even more difficult for me. I have found out that I can do it alone, but I want someone to hold my hand through the dark and hard parts. Not because I need it, but because I'm finally willing to allow that support in my life. I'm finally willing to admit that I want a true partnership that provides that harbor. But since it wasn't there, I've had to manage without it. And I do so quietly." He said nothing, and the subject was never reopened. Not on the ride home, not later that night in bed. It was as if I never said a word.

In our next session with Chapman, I told Keith again, but in different words, that I was exhausted from doing it all on my own and that I wanted a partner. I told him that I was capable of doing it all on my own. I said that he could go on working fourteen-hour days, not connecting with me, and not being in a partnership with me, and I could be a good wife and take care of the house and kids, but that there would be a price to pay in our marriage. I told him that I was afraid that after so many years of walking on my own, I might get to a place where I no longer needed or desired having him walk next to me. It was a threat.

He said nothing in response. And Chapman asked him, "Keith, do you understand what Carly is saying?" He shook his head, and I had to explain it again. And then Chapman took over and said, "Keith, what I think Carly is saying is that your marriage is in trouble, and while she is okay doing this all on her own, eventually, she is not going to need you as a partner anymore." Keith clenched his jaw the way he does when he is angry and still said nothing.

Chapman sent us home with an assignment. He identified that Keith needed to feel secure about our future, which is why he worked so much, so he wanted us to find a tangible action that we could take to help Keith feel like we were trying to take care of our future. Chapman also pointed out that I needed to feel secure about our present and that I wanted a connection now.

On the drive home, I suggested we start putting money every month into our retirement fund so we could feel less stressed about the future. I suggested that, for me, we could write each other letters once a week from work to reconnect as individuals and find intimacy again. He agreed. The money from the account was drawn each month, and I sent the first letter to his work. He never responded. When I asked him about it, he said he couldn't remember where he put it and he was planning on responding.

Then one afternoon in the summer of 2014, I got an email while I was at the dentist. It was from Christopher Jones. He said he was sorry that it took him so long to respond to my email. How meaningful my words were and how he thought of me often. How he wanted to know if I would be willing to be part of a documentary that a station in Utah was producing about Mitchell's Journey that could help so many people.

I was stunned. Me? My email? This man was one of my parenting heroes. He inspired change in the way I parented. Every time I "had to" do something that was annoying or challenging with one of my boys, I would think, *No, I get to. Chris and Natalie would kill for this.*

I wrote back and forth with Chris, and he put me in touch with the producer of the documentary, Candace, a woman who would also become a soul sister. At the end of the summer, Candace and her cameraman flew to Cleveland to interview me and record my family at our perfect house. They spent four hours interviewing and taping us playing in the backyard with the boys. Keith came home early from work to be part of it. It was an unforgettable time.

A year and a few days after I sent Chris that first email, the documentary came out. I proudly posted my small involvement in such a big movement on my Facebook page. Much love and support came my way, and the next morning, a single message appeared in my Facebook message inbox. The message was from Jonathan Agin. I knew his name instantly. It was a gut punch when I saw it. We were Facebook friends because he graduated from high school with Keith, but I barely knew him. What I did know of him registered immediately. He had lost his almost five-year-old girl, Alexis, to a fatal brain cancer that was similar to the one my uncle died of. And I also remembered hearing that his sister was killed in a tragic car accident. I remembered reading his entries about Alexis when they were going through that unimaginable hell and crying.

It was a long, and honest, and forthright letter about his impressions of me in the documentary and how he had no idea that we were going through what we were going through. And that if I wanted to share what was going on, he wanted to hear about it. Before I replied, I wrote to Christopher that he and Mitchell were connecting people who would have never been connected and how his little boy was reaching people all over the universe. Then I responded to Jonathan, meditated, and went about my day in awe and amazement. My world was opening in a way that felt light and meaningful.

Chapter 53:

A Message That Changed Everything

That first correspondence with Jonathan led to another and another. I told Keith about the new friendship that was organically growing and how cool it was. He hadn't spoken with Jonathan since high school, but he remembered him and was indifferent. While the medical challenges of our children were the organic topic that brought us together, our desire to talk, to ask questions, and to be brutally honest with each other kept us coming back for more. We quickly found out that we were like the male and female versions of each other. We were snarky and sarcastic and quick on our toes. One message a day became many messages throughout the day and a deep friendship grew.

We talked about our outlook, and our dreams, and our concept of God, and what we were afraid of, and what we wished we could try. About three weeks in, I was on my StairMaster watching a show called *Girlfriend's Guide to Divorce*, and I panicked because in the show the wife had been emailing with a guy and that started their divorce. The thought was like a flame I drew my hand back from. I jumped from the StairMaster and messaged Jonathan to tell him I couldn't talk to him anymore because I didn't want to get a divorce.

The next three days of no contact were tortuous and very telling. I was irritable, sad, confused, and lonely. I told Keith, on a walk, that I had stopped talking to Jonathan because we were becoming very emotionally close, and I didn't want to cause problems in our marriage. He looked at me and asked if I was going to sleep with Jonathan. I jokingly told him, "No, silly. He lives in D.C." And that was that. It was settled. Keith told me he didn't care if we had an emotional connection. He was actually relieved because he didn't want that kind of relationship with me. He told me as long as I wasn't going to sleep with him, we could be friends.

I couldn't get back to the house fast enough to message Jonathan. He admitted that he was shocked by how much of an impact he felt in the absence of our friendship. We continued to share our souls, bare our hearts, and open ourselves up to the truest friendship I have ever known. I felt guilty for feeling so much for a man I had never met, who was married with children, who lived in Virginia, who was becoming my best friend on earth.

I don't know who I had truly shared myself with before there was him. I don't think I shared myself on that level with anyone. I think he was the first and only person who completely and thoroughly wanted to know all of me and wanted me to know all of him. We played question games all the time. What's your favorite activity to do when you're alone? What dream do you have that you would be heartbroken if you never attempted? Who would you want to be trapped in an elevator with?

Over the next months, we motivated the other to find acceptance in our disintegrating marriages. We encouraged each other to seek therapy, try harder, read this, look at that, listen to this, try that, and we grew and grew. Our roots grew deeper, and our branches grew higher. Before we knew it, before it could be seen, the intertwining became inextricable deep under the surface.

Dear Christopher Jones,

Although we have never met in person, you show
up for me exactly when I need you. I was in the car
feeling so low and almost hopeless. Levi was sick,
and while I was usually optimistic, I was struggling
that day. And then you came crashing into my life.
You have a gift with words, and the very first post
I saw was the day your Mitchell passed away. You
changed my life. You helped me zoom out from
my pain to see your pain, gratitude, reminders,
heartache, and love. Being part of your documentary
was an honor I can never truly put into words. The
documentary aired, and my entire world changed.
You and your son brought people into my life that I
would never have known otherwise. There is never
a day I do not think of you. I run with your son's
name on my chest, and I climb with him in my
heart. Thank you for all you have given to this world.
Thank you for reminding me what really matters,
and thank you for having such a giving family that is
willing to share your light with all of us. I am forever
better because of you.

Chapter 54:

The Chasm

I messaged Jonathan: *You are the kind of man I wish I could have as my partner. But since we're both married and never want to get a divorce, I declare that you will become my best friend.*

He replied with a laughing emoji and the words, *You're crazy.* And without any effort on our part, a love developed without either one of us wanting or seeking it. Being the person I am, I struggled. I was in so much discomfort and pain. My heart, soul, and mind were at war. It was one of the most brutal struggles of my lifetime. Having taken those vows, even though it was nothing like what I wanted it to be, falling for someone else was totally incongruous with my values about marriage.

But once you know, you cannot unknow. Once you have seen behind the curtain, you cannot pretend you didn't see. As Jonathan often says, once the bullets are out of the gun, you cannot put them back in. I found myself Googling, *Should I stay for the kids?* I begged God to tell me what to do. I cried daily as I walked around my perfect house. My marriage included so many unproductive counseling sessions, three beautiful boys, no black eyes, no adultery, and no gambling, but I was dying inside every day.

I never knew how lonely one could be in a marriage, lying in bed next to another person, not touching, on our phones, millions of miles apart. He was a kind man and a good father. But I hungered for connection and wanting. Keith was quiet with a clenched jaw. We had these little kids and divorce would destroy them. And divorce would destroy him. So I chose to stay, over and over. And each day, a little piece of me died.

Sitting across from two of my closest girlfriends, they looked at me and said, "Your light went out." That was all I needed. I was trying to stay for the kids and for him, but in the process I had lost myself. Against the advice of family and friends, I left my perfect life and chose me.

Our divorce story was messy. And my story with Jonathan was what I call a beautiful mess. Where there had been darkness, loneliness, and brokenness came light, friendship, understanding, knowing, seeing, truth, soul voices, innocence, and love. From these stories has grown a new story. A story where two souls who would never have met found each other in the darkness and emerged holding hands.

During those final months of my marriage to Keith, I was trying to shove down what I knew was true. I made gratitude lists, forced myself not to feel how I felt, and begged everyone to tell me what I should do. But I was also speaking with my therapist, Chapman, and writing more than I had in years. When I was nineteen and newly sober, waiting in the waiting room for my appointment with Chapman, I used to climb out onto the fire escape, smoke, scribble in my journal, and try to see the world around me from a different perspective. Chapman has watched me grow, unfold, grapple with my truths, share my fears and my dreams. Those early sessions were my emotional boot camps that helped me become this unrelenting warrior of a woman. When I went back to him so many years later to help me figure out what the hell I was going to do about my marriage, he and I solved the problem in one session.

"I don't want to be married to him anymore. I am not in love with him, and I haven't been for years."

Chapman nodded and asked, "What do you want to do?"

Without any censorship, I blurted out, "I want to get a divorce, but I don't know how to do it."

"I have never seen anyone work as diligently and for as long as you have on making your marriage work. And I must admit that I was surprised it has taken you so long to get to this place."

In another session, one where I mostly hyperventilated and cried, I wrote this passage after getting off the phone with Chapman: *Our marriage is over, and I want a divorce. It is time for a dissolution. What would I look like if I was someone who trusts God? I would be calmer. I would pray and meditate. I would spread light. I would take the next needed action. I have fallen out of love with my husband. I no longer believe he is capable of showing up or supporting me emotionally in the future. My heart has taken a huge toll, and I'm ready to leave.*

I had reams of proof that I would most likely continue to do the bulk of parenting and medical care all by myself. While that weighed heavily on my chest, I also realized that if this trend continued, I would be left on my own for my personal medical care down the line as we grew older.

Dear Chapman,

> The winds of fortune blessed me with you as my
> therapist. When I met you at nineteen years old,
> I had already seen so many doctors. Most of them
> just scribbled, didn't look up, and barely listened to

what I was saying. But you called me out right up front on an issue I needed to hear, and I respected you immediately. We had some terrifying moments in the beginning when I told you how loud and destructive it was inside of my head. You told me that if it got really bad, I would need to check myself in somewhere to be safe. I can't believe I've been sitting in front of you on and off for twenty years, through so many of my life's experiences. When I think of the people who have helped shape me the most in my life, you are on the short list. I am so appreciative of your brutal honesty, your empathy, and your willingness to share your own humanity with me. I believe the reason I have turned out as I have has so much to do with many of the lessons you have taught me. I am most thankful for two specific gifts. The first was when we were preparing to take Levi to Boston Children's and possibly not bring him home. You told me that I was on a mission to save my baby boy and there was no time for emotions. That was crucial. The other was when I was struggling with the decision to divorce and you patiently walked with me through all the facts and helped me to see that I had already done so much legwork. I remember crying on the phone with you one afternoon when I knew what I needed to do and I was just so frightened of the outcome I could not see. Thank you for your kindness and guidance. It means more to me than you could ever know. I wish you only amazing adventures as you ride off on your motorcycle with your friends.

Dear Kevin,

There is a saying that when the student is ready, the teacher will appear. That's exactly what happened with you and me. I was thirteen years sober and could not find anyone who would lead me through the work. After hearing you speak at a meeting, I knew I needed to follow you around and learn from you. After much drama, rumors, and arguing in parking lots, you gave in and taught me how to help women. You changed how I do the work of recovery, how I do it with other women, and I've grown spiritually because of that. You are opinionated, outspoken, and committed to this sober path. I can relate to you. You have made me a better mother, guide, mentor, and human. Thank you for helping me continuously lay the junk in my brain out on the table and point out what might help and what might cause harm. You taught me how to use my voice and respectfully stand up for myself. We have walked down many tough roads in the years of our friendship, but no road has been more unchartered, dark, or wondrous as the one we are walking now. On August 17th, I received the worst call from you I could ever imagine. "Kayleigh is dead." From that night to this moment, I have been humbled to be your witness and friend. I promised you that I would never let you walk alone. And I meant that. I love watching the spiritual and sacred relationship you and Kayleigh created. Thank you for your humanity. Thank you for sharing your deepest pain with me. I am forever changed.

Chapter 55:

Your Own Oxygen Mask

In the last months of my marriage, I was diagnosed with a scary, potentially life-altering condition. I had to go to a crucial medical appointment two hours away, and Keith not only didn't come with me, but he hadn't even remembered I was going. When I called to check on the boys, he asked me where I had been all day. My mom was in the car with me and overheard the conversation. I was embarrassed that my husband so clearly didn't care about me. I was humiliated and angry. I looked into my future with him and felt afraid he would keep pulling away from me while I go through aging and illness because it's too much for him. He'll think I'm "damaged." When I told him about my medical issue, he had that look on his face that was a cross between annoyed and righteous. He said, "Given your childhood, I understand why your belly is so messed up." It made me want to cry and scream at him. Why couldn't he just give me a big hug and tell me he loves me and he'll be there for me no matter what? Or that he's sorry that he hadn't been there?

I continued to search for the strength to trust God's guidance through this decision. I uttered this prayer daily, over and over: "God, if it's your will for us to be together, put us together. God, if it's your will for us to stay apart, keep us apart. God if it's your will for me to not know today, keep me not knowing." It was one of the most difficult prayers I've ever said. I could hardly get through the days at work without my uncle Jerry sitting by my side. We worked together and his calm presence and practical guidance kept me breathing and focusing on whatever was next in front of me.

Keith knew about my feelings and connection with Jonathan. I had been completely honest in therapy. While he never believed that nothing had physically happened between us, he and the last marriage therapist were convinced if I would just stop communicating with Jonathan, our marriage would get back on track.

During one of those dark silences between me and Jonathan, Keith and I went on a couples retreat with our temple. In that idyllic setting, I forced myself to recommit to my marriage. It was what I imagine gay conversion camp must be like. I made the decision to not feel anything at all and just stay for the kids.

I thought making this choice would make the pain go away, and then I would be able to go back to my regular life and not feel so tortured inside. But my heart only wanted Jonathan. I would spend all day trying to convince myself to stay with Keith. I could be pretty convincing, but then I would be haunted by Jonathan's honesty, emotional availability, and sensitivity. There was so much that was shared, there was so much that was promised. And Jonathan would message back, responding to whatever fears I left in his inbox. "Dive into the waves. Never let your fear decide your fate."

I wrote to him, *I love what you said to me the other day, about running away from you because of my fears.*

He wrote, *Carly, my dear, don't run from me. You've let me see inside your soul, and I know you can't turn away from your truth once you know it. And I can't turn away from you, ever. Got it?*

I loved his raw confidence. His bold words lit me up from within. He would bravely place himself right in front of my heart, calling out how I was being mistreated and how I deserve to be loved. His strength and his flaws looked amazing on him. He would tell me, "I cannot imagine my life without you." I felt exactly the same way. In my car, the song "Riptide" frequently came on, which we both loved. I would see bikers and runners that reminded me of all of the races he did, and I felt like I could not escape him. He haunted me.

Chapman and I came to the conclusion that I could not turn against my heart. If I had put a gun to my head at any point during those brutal, gut-wrenching months of back and forth between my heart and my mind, I always knew what I would do. When I looked in the mirror, I always saw the truth. I could hide it in a picture, or mask it in a post, but the mirror never lied. When we live our lives with authenticity, mistakes, and beautiful messes, all that is left is the light.

Right before the end of my marriage to Keith, we went to San Francisco to celebrate our tenth wedding anniversary. I didn't want to go, but I willed myself. It had been planned for a while. It felt like an excruciating exercise of going through the motions. I had already told Keith how I felt. I told him how hungry I was for connection and how lonely I had become. We had been to three different marriage counselors by then and nothing was helping.

On the airplane, I felt like we were hurtling toward our end. I decided I needed a reminder to have enough courage to handle whatever was ahead. As soon as there was service on the plane, I Googled tattoo shops in the vicinity of our hotel. Half a block away was Moth and Dagger. When we got to San Francisco, I had the words "God has you" inked onto my skin on the inside of my left arm, printed upside down so only I could read it. Now, every time I felt afraid, I could look at my arm and remember I was not alone and that God had me no matter what.

Dear Jerry,

We have always had a special bond out of all of our family members, even when I was a little girl. I remember Siesta Key visits on my own in your house with freedom to roam the island, and fresh croissants from your market, and scary rated R movies late at night. Thank you for always being level with me and telling me what you see in me that makes me special. Thank you for showing me how to behave in the restaurant business and how to treat every single person from the chef to the dishwasher with equal kindness and to learn all of their names. I always feel like you really want to know me and celebrate who I am. That makes me feel seen and heard and understood. On one of my stays with you, when I got to work in your restaurant and watch you work your magic with your customers and employees, you gave me a card that meant more than you could know. It was simple, but its message was clear. You wrote, *The more I know you, the more I love you*, and I believed you because you have always taken the time to know me. And that is one of the gifts I hope gets passed down to me from you. I want people to

feel how I feel in your presence. But what I truly
want to thank you for is sitting next to me at
work, five days a week, for all of these painful years
of indecision, custody crap, house hunting, and
family drama. You have been my voice of reason
and my internal compass. You don't just listen to
my problems, you come back the next day and
share what I might have missed and point out a
different way to look at my options. You are one
of my closest humans and I could never fathom
making my way without your unwavering love and
judgement-free guidance.

Dear Sarah,

There is no other relationship in my life where
there is such symbiosis. We began together with me
helping you and then it effortlessly shifted into you
helping me. I feel equal, understood, and respected
in your presence. You say it like it is, and you never
pretend to be okay when you're not. That makes
for the kind of friendship that will hopefully last
a lifetime. You are the closest female friend in my
life, and we have both shared all our skeletons,
fears, regrets, and embarrassing medical issues.
Being the officiant at your wedding was one of the
greatest honors of my life. Thank you for telling
me to stop calling my sons "pussy," because pussies
are strong, life-giving, and resilient, and the way
I was using that word was not accurate; instead,
you coached me to tell them to stop being such
"ball sacks" because testicles are fragile and delicate.
Thank you for sitting next to me on the picnic table

in the Metro Parks and allowing me to shed all of my tears, ugly thoughts, and secrets, and for never judging me or putting your own agenda on mine. I love watching you unfold and become the mother and partner I always knew you would be. I believed in your dreams more than you did the same way you believed in mine. I love you more.

Chapter 56:

Rocking Chairs

We were in each other's physical presence for the first time at a diner in an old trolley car in Bethesda with children all over the place. I was visiting the NIH with Levi for our third time. When I first found out about the upcoming visit, I messaged Jonathan the dates and secretly hoped he would be traveling. I was afraid to come face-to-face with this man I had been falling in love with every day for so long. Our marriages were falling apart, and I needed to not be falling for him.

He was in town and would meet us for dinner with his two boys. I was so nervous that I had to take one of my stomach pills to release the spasms in my belly. Levi was so excited that we were going to go out with other kids. The previous time, it had been just the two of us, and as much fun as I am, he craves the energy of someone his age. He brought treats from the snack table to give to Jonathan's boys. I prayed that I would not be physically attracted to Jonathan, so I could put all these feelings behind me, and we could just be super close friends.

Jonathan picked us up. I laughed nervously as I got Levi situated in the car and buckled myself in. I looked over at Jonathan and knew I was screwed. He was so good-looking. He was so much better looking in person. And now he was sitting next to me in a car with our kids laughing in the back seat, and we were driving in Bethesda. The electricity between us was almost visible. Even the kids picked up on it. His son kept asking, "Dad, are you okay?" We looked at each other and smiled as he answered over and over again that he was fine.

In the restaurant, the boys colored on their kids' menus, and we tried to play War. When the cards fell on the floor, I went under the table to gather them, and I looked up to see Jonathan smirking at me. I had never felt anything like this in my life. He made me feel exposed. This man knew more about me than anyone had. We had bared our souls to each other and shared everything. And here we were, in a diner, with chicken fingers, apple sauce, dry mouths, and beating hearts.

It was late, but the boys wanted to come see the playroom at The Children's Inn that Levi was so excited to share. We ended up in the second-floor playroom, sitting on rocking chairs opposite each other as our boys laughed and got into trouble for being too loud. Jonathan warned his kids that they were leaving in two minutes over and over again.

We sat there rocking, staring at each other. There was nothing else to say. My hands gripped the wooden arms of the rocking chair, and my feet bounced as we stared deep into each other's eyes. No one had ever looked that deeply into my soul. In fact, I had never allowed another man to look into my eyes like that without turning away. I concentrated on his blue eyes that were piercing me. He could see everything, and he smiled and never looked away. I saw in his eyes a man who had become my best friend and my go-to person for all things upsetting, silly, boring, and secretive.

I could hear our boys making up games and bossing each other around, but all I could do was look in Jonathan's eyes. I could feel that he wanted to kiss me. I wanted him to kiss me.

But we were not in a position to kiss each other. Not that night or ever, as far as I was concerned. I forced myself to breathe and was only interrupted by two of our kids announcing that they needed to go to the bathroom.

That night, we never touched. We didn't even hug good-bye. In fact, we would never touch until we were both free. But in those rocking chairs, we solidified the unspoken feelings that were bubbling inside us both.

Chapter 57:

The Tooth Fairy Isn't Real

I left my second marriage counselor in tears and sat with Elana in her car. I cried because I thought I could never leave my marriage because of the kids. She asked me a question that no one had ever asked before: "Are you in love with Jonathan?"

I stopped crying for a moment, looked at her, and said matter-of-factly, "What does it matter? I can't do anything about my feelings anyway." But that question unlocked the gates of truth inside of me. And once I know something, I can't unknow it.

That little kernel of truth started to peel away everything I couldn't admit before. After I got home, I called Jonathan and said, "I have a problem."

Like he always did when I brought anything to him, he anxiously asked, "What's wrong?"

My heart was racing, and I blurted it all out. "I'm in love with you, and everything is a mess, and I don't know what to do."

He didn't say, "Carly, I'm flattered, but we can't go there."

He didn't say, "This is really inappropriate. We're friends."

I don't even recall what he did say. All I know is everything changed after those rocking chairs.

There was no more holding back our truths after that. Within a few weeks, Jonathan and I lay out a dream that seemed inconceivable. It was the highest and most dangerous cliff either of us had ever approached. If one of us jumped off, would the other take a step back or would they join us below?

When we made the decision to end our marriages and to craft a love story that did not make logistical sense but made soul sense, we were met with judgement, anger, confusion, and hateful words. But I found even those to be gifts. Even though I was experiencing that isolating pain of receiving approval only from myself and God, those brutal months were my unraveling, my becoming, and my renaissance. I arrived at a place where I realized that anyone's reaction to my truth was not any of my business.

Jonathan and I did not leave our marriages because of each other. We left because our marriages were individually irreparable. We had both found that when both partners do not want the same life, it makes for an extremely lonely existence.

Chapman challenged me, saying, "If you would really leave regardless of what Jonathan does or doesn't do, then prove it. Don't have contact with him. Just take care of yourself." He reminded me, "You have walked through hell and back and have emerged stronger and closer to God. There's nothing you can't walk through. You are never alone."

So I made the decision to cut off contact with Jonathan while we each did what we had to do in our marriages. Instead of planning to end up together, I told him we would each follow our hearts and see where that led. I left before Jonathan did. I struggled to not talk to him while he was going through his mess of an ending, but I knew that just because I had set myself free, it didn't mean it was right for me to interfere with him while he was sorting out his ending. I finally got to a place where I couldn't lie anymore to myself or anyone else, where I had to honor within what I knew needed to be done and that was to live a life without lying. I had come too far to lie about any part of my life.

Instead of communicating with him, I continued to write in my journal everything I would usually share with him. I resisted the urge to reach out to him. I was determined not to muddy it up. I wanted to feel proud, and humble, and honest. I didn't want to lie to anyone. No more lies. To anyone. None. I wanted to live a life where the only judges were God and myself. I was making the decision to make a new agreement. To live in a way that was true. To not go against myself and what feels authentic.

Because I left before he did, there was a very real possibility that he would be too afraid to dive into the waves. I could see myself having torn apart my entire world and then receiving a message telling me he just couldn't go through with it. Even though that would have been incredibly painful, it would have been completely logical. Regardless, leaving was the right choice for me. I needed to let go and trust. I needed to act like someone whose God gives her what she needs and not always what she wants.

Through much therapy, writing, prayer, meditation, crying, and begging, Jonathan and I chose to listen to our souls. The voices within each of us told us, individually, that the other was our favorite person, our best friend, and our soul mate. We knew what was ahead would be rough. We would be living a most untraditional life in two different states, caring for our two separate families as single parents. But what we had found in each other was unlike anything we had even known was possible.

Our strengths were complementary. My strong spirit and unwavering conviction complemented his honesty and bravery in confronting his fears. The universe used him to teach me so many lessons. I have never known a man who considered me to be so full of light and wisdom. He was attracted to every part of me like I was to him. We believed in each other and fell in love with each other's scars.

After many painful weeks of no contact, Jonathan reached out to me and told me he had left.

We went through the devastating processes of disassembling our marriages, houses, and schedules. We were devoted to standing hand in hand in the waves of life together. Our promise was to love the other and the other's children, to come together throughout our strange and challenging parenting schedules, and to push the other to pursue their dreams.

We were mostly winging it and editing our stories as we went. We were both in tremendous discomfort in our own ways, but we were finally living our truths with gratitude and perspective. We became a partnership that unapologetically loves the path we have chosen while respecting the other's messes and journey.

Early on in this process, I was sitting with my friend, Scott—one of my lighthouses who had been divorced for years and was happy and living a purposeful life. Scott guided me through my divorce. He gave me one of my greatest gifts: The concept of the North Star. He told me that my boys needed to be the North Star for me and their father. That we would wander off as we attempted to sail the rocky, unpredictable waters of divorce, but a bright North Star would keep us from getting too far off course. I loved that idea so much that I had it tattooed on my inner forearm to remind me.

Keith and I used this metaphor to tell our boys about the divorce. We explained that when sailors lose their way, they look up and focus on that constant star, the only tool that can guide them in the dark. We told them that they were our North Star and that when we didn't know what to do, we would think of what's best for them to decide the next right move. This brought me and Keith back again and again when we wanted to stand our ground and stubbornly dig our heels in. It brought us back to the moment. Back to our focus.

Our boys were our North Star, and their story of divorce would not be written by the tweets and comments of onlookers who were angry and stuck as victims. Their story of divorce would be written by their mom and dad, and we chose to put aside our resentments and pain to construct a new story. To avoid getting off course, sailors need to know two things: where they were and where they are going.

It was not easy. There were times when I wanted to sail headfirst into an iceberg, but then the questions would tug at my heart. What do I want to teach my boys about love? About forgiveness? About patience? Instead, I decided to compose a new story, and the only response I have about my role as a mother is this: I mess up, I lose my temper, I forget important items, I have been known to swear, and I am silly and inappropriate. But one question I can always answer with an unequivocal yes: am I a good mother?

Divorce has been one of the greatest sources of loneliness, pain, freedom, growth, stretching, and pushing that I've ever experienced. People often message me quietly for help on how to navigate this treacherous minefield. I am not the divorce whisperer. I am not an expert. But I have my experience and my story, and this path has placed me in the way of beauty, sadness, and strength.

Early on, I called my friend and guide, Kevin, while crying outside of the tattoo parlor in San Francisco. I had my newly-inked tattoo, "God has you," all wrapped and burning with tears running down my cheeks. I remember asking him what was wrong with me. He laughed and told me, "You're having a renaissance."

There were no more secrets, no more wrapping paper, and no more perfect Facebook posts. The legal process of divorce was full of brutal emails, plotting, and living together while trying to sell our dream home. Those months included the most exhausting spiritual work of my life, but the only way out of the shit tunnel was through. And through I traveled.

Except for trips to Boston for Levi's head, or Bethesda for the NIH, or one trip with Keith, I had never left my children, ever. With the divorce proceeding and everything out in the open with Keith, I took my first weekend away to San Francisco to meet Jonathan on the opposite end of the United States. I had Cheryl Strayed's *Tiny Beautiful Things,* my journal, and a desperate hunger to find my way back to me.

I remember seeing a meme on Facebook by Anonymous, that said, "Unfuck yourself: Be who you were before all that stuff happened that dimmed your fucking shine." I felt like someone had climbed inside my body and put in a new LED light bulb. I felt like the doctor had finally given me the correct prescription for my lenses. I could finally see again.

Dear Scott,

> I knew you only from Facebook the night I
> messaged you and asked for help. But the universe
> told me to reach out to you, and I no longer
> ignore the universe's directions. One evening

of storytelling has turned into a soul-sibling friendship. Thank you for sharing all of your stories with me and recognizing when a moment was open and calling us both. Thank you for telling me about the North Star and being my lighthouse. Thank you for empowering me to use this intense experience to get closer to the woman, parent, and human I want to become. I love our nightly commitment of sharing five moments we are grateful for during each day. That exchange is so vulnerable and connecting. In those messages, we give each other glimpses of our day and where we found something to be grateful for. We are going on year three, and we have promised to exchange gratitude until one of us is no longer here. Thank you for teaching me about giving myself permission to be human and empowering me to craft my own life. You are one of my trusted go-to teachers. I love you. Thank you for helping me find my light again.

Chapter 58:

You Can't Always Get What You Want

There were so many inspiring words out there that I would cling to, but the line that rang true for me most of all was Robert Frost's "The only way out is through." And Christopher Jones added, "There are no shortcuts." I can confirm that there aren't, I have looked for them. There is no way around the pain, the work, the effort, and the perception shifts needed to pull ourselves out and through. The abnormal became our new normal. The boys began to learn whose weekend it was.

Kissing my boys and sending them off with their dad is tough. Not getting to be there for each and every moment sucks. Jonathan always reminds me, "This path is not for the faint of heart." Just because I might be smiling and laughing doesn't mean that this choice is free from challenges, obstacles, and pain. But what path is?

I have been asked countless times to alleviate the fear of pain from those starting down the road of divorce, but I cannot. I once lived a life that was not fully honest, but I no longer wrap up the truth to make it easier to digest. I tell whoever is asking, "There is no easy path whatever choice you make. Staying or leaving will both require work, sacrifice, fear, and pain. Our children will be affected either way."

Many are in the delusion that if they stay, everything will be all better. Or if they leave, everything will fall into place. But it isn't so black and white; nothing is that simple. I was reminded of this truth right after we moved to our new separate homes. My sweet, quiet Franklin came to me and admitted, "I'm sad that my parents don't live in the same house. I was afraid to tell you because I was scared you would be upset by my feelings." I heard my own heart break, but I did what I knew was right. I focused on the North Star and called his father, so we could all process it together. Because we do our best to focus on our boys, my son was able to have both his parents help him through.

I realized that I had been trying to create a world where my son would be free of pain. But that world does not exist. And then it hit me. The pain is the teacher. The pain is how we grow closer to God, closer to others, closer to our truest selves. I thought of my own childhood and how it was not free of pain and how that pain helped me become who I am today. How Levi, with two potentially fatal medical conditions, taught me how to be the mother I am today. How the strongest and bravest people I know are those who are walking through unimaginable hallways, and how they only become more radiant and more real as they continue to walk.

I don't have a magical answer for what anyone should do in their struggle. I only know that the soul needs to grow. And for that, like photosynthesis, the soul needs light. I lean towards the light as I keep walking through. As Rumi said, "The cure for the pain is in the pain."

Dear Divorce, you strong bitch,

You are the hardest teacher I've ever had. You're also the best. You kicked my ass hard in the beginning.

The pain and the fear were almost too much to bear. But the gifts just keep coming. In no special order, I thank you for making me a better parent. I found out how capable I am. I found my voice and get tons of opportunities to use it. I no longer live in a perfect house with a desperately lonely life. I found strength within myself that I truly did not know was available. You have brought me soul friends. You have forced me to be okay with myself regardless of what anyone else thinks. You have shown me how to step back and see the panoramic view. You have taught me empathy. You have taught me that no one actually knows what's really going on in anyone's marriage. You've taught me not to judge other people's marriages. You have helped me understand there is no such thing as "wanting" a divorce, because no one wants this. You taught me that the outcome of the marriage depends on both partners' involvement, or lack thereof, that no one is truly at fault except in extreme cases. You have given me permission to be human during the terrible moments, the moments where I miss my kid terribly, the moment I wish I had a partner at curriculum night, and all the rest. But you are my best teacher because I have become, I am unfolding, I am bursting open from your endless lessons. Thank you for teaching me. Thank you for believing in me more than I believe in myself.

Chapter 59:

I Run for Those Who Can't

As Jonathan and I started blending our worlds together and sharing the cards we had been dealt, I laid my biggest card on the table: Levi. I needed to know if Jonathan was willing to love another kid with serious medical conditions. I didn't need to know if he could do it, I already knew he was a capable partner, father, and advocate for medically fragile kids. I needed to know, "Will you do this with me, knowing the toll it takes on your heart, the fear, the changing of plans at the last moment? Are you really willing to take all this on, after losing Alexis? Are you willing to love Levi and help me navigate this?"

He didn't hesitate. "I promise you could have no better partner by your side."

And he has been true to his word. He has been with us to the NIH and has contacted important medical people on Levi's behalf. When the first painful shot wasn't enough during one of Levi's flare-ups, when Levi was limp, pale, feverish, and scared, Jonathan did exactly what we needed him to do. He warmed the injection in his hand, researched ways to make it less painful, and held Levi down while he screamed. I need to remember to trust that voice within me about people. To believe that voice when it tells me who to bet on.

One of the reasons I know God saved me is so I could be the mother to these three boys. I love my boys madly. They are each their own little humans, but Levi is my karma baby in temperament, energy, and naughtiness. When the Children's Inn, the safe haven where we stay for free when we go to the NIH, asked me to raise funds and run a 10K for them, what else could I say other than, "Of course."

Since the divorce, I've kept a bucket list and challenged myself to get out of my comfort zone. I wrote an article to fundraise for Levi's 10K as I logged miles:

> "*Your son's fevers are not compatible with life.*"
>
> "*Do you know how many minutes it would take for your son to bleed out on an operating table?*"
>
> "*Your son is a rare bird.*"
>
> "*Your son is a unicorn.*"
>
> "*Your son is a patient population of one.*"

These are some of the memorable one-liners I've heard while mothering Levi. And then there are the meetings I get to have with principals, babysitters, local rescue departments, and Levi's friends' parents to prepare those around him for what will hopefully never happen to his head if he cracks it open while under their care, all the while smiling and trying not to scare anyone away from him. And then there are the emergency room visits where I know more about my son's medical conditions than the medical professionals caring for him.

But then there is the National Institutes of Health. The researchers and clinicians there are so incredibly smart and attuned to cases like Levi's, and they are willing to tell me that they don't know what is wrong but not to give up. Within the NIH is my son's version of Disney

World: The Children's Inn, where his face lights up when he walks into the lobby and searches his mailbox to see what prizes have been left for his discovery. Where he walks around like a king, narrating his way through the playrooms and kitchens, stuffing donuts in his mouth and flopping on the bed in our room. Where he is so proud to be amongst the bravest of the brave. Where he learned firsthand why we can't stare at kids who are outwardly different. Where he played with an eight-year-old little boy whose mother was told he wouldn't make it to ten.

You see, Levi gets it. He knows more than a little boy should know. He knows to ask for something to squeeze as they take thirty vials of blood, boasting to the phlebotomist that he doesn't cry when he gets his weekly injections from Mom. The Inn is his other home. It is where he feels a part of. Where even though he doesn't look like one of the "sick kids," he still knows what it feels like to be one of them. And what Levi is most proud of right now is his mom because she (yes, I) has pledged to run the Marine Corps 10K, a race to raise money and awareness for families that come from all over to stay at the Inn while they walk the long halls searching for answers, on The Children's Inn team.

There are no ribbons for what my son has. He is undiagnosed. When the doctors hear hoofbeats, they are trained to think of a horse and not a zebra. But Levi is a zebra. They don't make races or bracelets for zebras.

This is the first time I have come across anything that directly benefits children like my son. Did I mention I hate running? Did I mention that I raised my goal so Levi could feel the support? But Levi hates bloodwork. And doesn't really love to miss school because he's only

253

a first grader and still loves to go. He hates wearing his helmet on the playground because he knows he looks different. So, I'm going to run for my son and all the families like ours. I'm going to show up for him and let him know that we grow stronger from our weaknesses. That our challenges are actually our blessings. That even if we don't know what is wrong with him, and I don't have any answers just yet, that there are people out there rooting for us and paving the way. While one more race and one more donation might not be the change that will fix all these broken pieces, it will make a difference to rare birds like Levi.

That run ended up being one of the most sacred moments of my life. I welled up running with Jonathan, alongside gold star families and mothers and fathers wearing pictures of their fallen children. We saw all of the marines rooting us on as I made my way with my runner's knees, braces, and gratitude for being able to run for those who couldn't.

I wore a shirt with so many names: Levi, Alexis, Mitchell, Kayleigh, Chase. The names of children who needed the Children's Inn to survive or those who lost their lives, leaving devastated parents behind. Through my pain and their pain, I ran for those who couldn't. And I was proud of myself and all the strength and beauty that was everywhere I looked.

Dear courageous lady at the Portland airport,

I'm so relieved that you were in the security line the night I hit a low bottom as a human. The train was late and it took forever to get to the airport for my red-eye flight from Portland to Cleveland. I needed to grab Levi and fly out the next afternoon to take him to the NIH. Because of the insane airport rules, I was not able to check my bag because I wasn't at the ticket counter to verify my ticket. The lines were extremely long. The security people did not care at all. I kindly begged them to contact the gate. I still had an hour before my plane left. They refused. They said I would have to try to carry it on and go through security. I had the unfortunate opportunity to go up to every single passenger and plead with them to let me go ahead of them. With tears in my eyes as I realized I might miss the flight and not be able to take Levi to the NIH, panic set in. The strangers were mostly kind, but the security people had zero interest in my story and said my suitcase was too large to carry on. I told them to take it. I would remove my toiletries and just give up all of my belongings. They said I'm not allowed to do that and that I would need to go all the way outside of the airport to leave my luggage and then start over through the line. I cried and said I would miss my flight, and they told me to move over so the next person could get through. I hyperventilated. I got on my knees—a grown woman, a mother, afraid of not being able to show up for her son—and ugly cried in front of 200 passengers and fifteen security people. No one did anything. But then you did. You were the only one who spoke up. You went to the security guards who were laughing at me and yelled that they should be ashamed of themselves. Couldn't they see how distraught I was? They were silent for a few moments then resumed laughing. I paid $950 for the next flight out and went through security a second time. I saw you near my new gate, and

I told you that your standing up for me meant everything. I keep getting to learn this lesson. That humans standing up for humans is all God wants from us. Thank you. I will never forget you, and whenever I am in line at the airport, I always let a frazzled stranger go ahead of me.

Chapter 60:

Regret Nothing

Shortly after moving in to our new home and becoming the kind of woman who other women came to for permission and inspiration, I was asked to write a piece that made me physically cringe, which was how I knew I had to do it. They had reached out to me because of my earlier pieces on divorce. The assignment was to write a letter to my former self on the eve of my wedding.

Dear Blushing Bride,

Regret nothing. You are twenty-six, beautiful, and full of hope.

Your parents gave you a fairy-tale wedding. All of the plans, details, centerpieces, and flower arrangements culminated in an unforgettable day.

If a genie came to you the night before and woke you from your sleep to reveal what would happen in your marriage, things might be different now.

Out of fear and ignorance, you would not have gone through with the wedding if you had known it would end in divorce elven years later.

But hindsight is not always 20/20. It does not take

into account the minute details, the lessons learned, the perspective, the challenges, or the joy. Oh, beautiful Carly, if you hadn't married Keith, you would have missed out on so much.

If a crystal ball showed you how this would end, you might not have gone through with it at all. You consider divorce to be a failure. I am here to tell you what has come from this union could never be considered a failure.

Today, you have three beautiful children because of this marriage. This marriage brought you to the place where you currently stand: a thirty-seven-year-old, newly single mother who's co-parenting with a man who you once wanted to spend the rest of your life with. The details of why you divorced are not up for discussion. Never allow anyone to call this marriage a failure. This marriage is not a failure.

Life simply happened. Life has a way of taking us down paths we never intended or expected. Life has a way of changing how we see everything. Those three beautiful children are gifts from the universe. Those three beautiful children are half of you and half of their father. Never forget this when you look at their faces. They are your North Star. Let them always guide you. If you focus on them, you will never stray off course.

Walk down that aisle. No regrets, girlfriend, no regrets. God has you.

Love,

Carly, age 37

God blessed me by matching me with Jonathan. He is the only man who has been willing to stand his ground, fight with me, look me in the eyes, and never walk away. On the night of our private wedding, we secluded ourselves in a cabin, laying side by side while the storm outside pounded and whistled. But even up until the moment when we separated to put on our wedding clothes, I still felt fear.

While he had given me no reason to doubt him, I came from a home where I could not trust that the people I loved would always be there. Then I matched with guys who couldn't see my worth. Because of all of this, I became a woman who never truly gave her heart to anyone but her boys. But on that porch during a humid summer night in July, we stood facing each other with our folded vows, and our nervous laughter, and three lit candles: one for Alexis, one for Mitchell, and one for Levi, the three children that brought us together. I knew it was time to give him all of my heart. And I have, but our wise spiritual healer of an officiant, Brenda, warned us that there would be winters of our marriage and that we had to hold hands and stick together.

There have been winters, and I know there will be more. The logistics are complicated with us living in two different states, with seven kids between us, co-parenting, working, handling finances, and being delayed at airports constantly. It's a challenge, and when things get uncomfortable, my modus operandi is to run. I look around and consider what I'd need to grab before running away. I imagine living alone and pretending this was all a dream. But Jonathan has grown to know that I am a mixture of so many truths. To know that I want my equal rights, but I also want the door held open for me. He recognizes the look on my face when I am ready to bolt and tells me that he is faster and stronger than I am, and if I make a run for it, he will track me down and never let me go. The truth is that I need him more than I pretend I don't.

One of Jonathan's amazing traits is that he responds almost instantly to all forms of communication, and if he can't talk, he messages me that he's on a call. One day, I couldn't reach him the entire day and hadn't heard a peep from him since 12:08 p.m. I began to worry. I texted and called, but none of my texts were "read" and none of my calls were answered. This wasn't like him.

Hours passed, and I reached out to his mom and his friends on Facebook. I considered calling hospitals and the police. I prayed that his phone was just broken. I panicked that he was in an accident and then realized that no one would even know to contact me. He finally answered eight hours later, saying he'd been at the beach all day without his phone. This was the first time his response was so delayed, and I told him to call his mom because I was too upset to talk.

I realized then I needed him more than I told myself I did. I also needed him to notify me if he was going to be unreachable because he has a wife with a very vivid imagination. Life is too precious and short to pretend we are okay on our own.

Dear Jonathan,

> I will never know why you chose to send me that message, but that one pebble in the pond made a ripple that would completely alter the rest of our lives. I've never known someone so convicted, committed, and able to bare his soul, cry his tears, and love me in every way a woman wants to be loved. This life with you is worth more than all the riches anyone could have. Thank you for your

living example of never allowing fear to decide your fate. I have done more bucket list items since you came crashing into my life than ever before. You are my better half. I will walk anywhere with you. No one makes me smile like you do. I get on my knees and thank God every day that you are the man you said you would be. Most people who know our story questioned either out loud or in their head, "How are they going to make this work?" I live in Cleveland, and you live in Virginia. You have your kids, and I have mine. How will this work? We used to try to assure people we would make it work, but then we just gave up, held hands, and faced each wave as it came. I know I am not easy to deal with or take care of. I'm stubborn, noncompliant, and have a difficult time staying still. But you show up and help create Halloween swords, teach the boys soccer tricks, and talk to the boys about all things male. You fly so often to see me and brave the Cleveland weather. Thank you for never saying I was too much. Thank you for being my best friend, my partner in crime, and my favorite person. I am a better human because of you. This life is messy, loud, and nonstop, but there's no one on earth I would rather hold hands with in the waves than you.

Chapter 61:

An Unapologetic Life

Because life is so short, I was so grateful to be influenced by Christopher Jones, Mitchell's father, who describes himself as an unapologetic photographer. With his permission, I have become an unapologetic photographer too. He took pictures of Mitchell through all the unbearable and beautiful times and made me realize it is not only acceptable to capture those moments, it is our lifeblood.

Something about snapping a picture during an ugly life moment seems politically incorrect. But those ugly moments are often, also, our most sacred moments, and those snapshots become priceless. I have taken them of Levi when he is sick or in a procedure to document, remember, refocus, and show all of our life, not just the highlight reel. With Christopher's permission, I knew what I had to do when I received my mom's call, and she was screaming into the phone, "Papa Harry is dead!"

I was in the turning lane at a busy intersection. My boys were in the back, as quiet as I've ever heard them. They had just heard my mom's voice on Bluetooth telling me, "The ambulance came, and I don't think he was alive." We would meet her at the hospital.

I sat at that stoplight and tried to imagine a world without my papa. It turned out that he would not make it to the ER alive. When it was my turn to sit with him and say goodbye, I picked up his hand and held it.

I remember, as a little girl, holding his big hand and wondering if he enjoyed holding my little hand. I wondered if being with me brought him the taste of a youth he was never able to have. As I sat there, holding his hand for the final time, I picked up my phone and took a picture. That picture is the single most important picture I have ever taken. Christopher, Mitchell, and Papa Harry helped me to take that picture. We will never regret the ones we take. We only regret the ones we wished we had taken.

I walk on the balance beam feeling scared and wobbly, and I hesitate to take the next step. I feel God's strong hand and hear God's clear voice say, "I've got you." I take another slow and careful step, then pause and look back. I feel God's hand, and I hear God's voice say, "I've got you."

There were more hard lessons ahead. That first year on my own after my divorce from Keith was the kind of teacher no one wanted. The kind of teacher you begged your mom to call your school about and get your classes switched so you could have a different teacher. But I got her and she was tough. She pushed me. She asked me to take action I never thought I could or would. She was merciless at times, but she believed in me just enough to take me further than any teacher had before. And isn't it the tough teachers who teach us the most?

We moved into a new home, neighborhood, and life. Keith moved four blocks away, and we started co-parenting. It went well for the most part, as long as we placed the North Star above all else. This was not always easy with significant others, rumors, and sticky subjects, but none of that really matters if we are focusing on the boys.

Our new home would turn one hundred years old shortly after we moved in. It came with charm and lessons all its own. I scrubbed the pots and killed the stink bugs that I had once left for my ex to handle. I called for help when digital issues were beyond my capabilities. But as a family, we grew under that first year's heavy arm.

Together, the four of us created a new system. My boys now had real chores that not only helped our house function better and relieved me of some of the many, many jobs, but that would also help grow them into the kind of men I wanted them to become. We got a bunch of popsicles and a deep freezer for the garage and quickly made new friends. We have more of a laid-back philosophy on many things that used to matter so much. They taught me that socks do not have to be paired or folded. They taught me that there is no point in turning their clothes from inside out to outside in. Before, it seemed like everything needed to appear perfect.

We read, we play, we have cereal for dinner when the day takes more out of us then we can give back. There are penises drawn on all of the mirrors. We have a sign in the house that says, "Always be yourself, unless you can be Batman. Then you should always be Batman," hanging in the kitchen and another in the living room that reads, "There are two kinds of business: my business and none of my business."

On the stairs leading up to our rooms is a poem I wrote them telling them to leave the world lighter than how they found it and to come home if they get lost because I will be here waiting. I have the Four Agreements painted on old shutters and hanging on a wall to remind us never to take anything personally. My old armoire was transformed into a bright pink pantry full of snacks for the boys and their friends.

That first year taught me to let go of anger that no longer served me. To let go of the façade of a perfect life and let my beautiful mess be seen without fear of judgement. I would teach them through my humanity instead of my attempts to be perfect. They expected that after Mom pulled out of the driveway, she would most likely pull right back in and run into the house to grab her phone or purse that she had forgotten. And that it was okay. She's doing her best.

That first year was the teacher who demanded me to be better, stronger, and more real than any other teacher ever had. She also loved me enough to give me the community, strength, and love I needed to be the mom my boys need. As many on social media have memed how excited they were to see her end, I looked back on that first year with exhaustion and gratitude for all she gave me.

For Mother's Day that first year on my own, Levi wrote me a card. *Dear Mom, Thank you for being my mom. Thank you for sticking up for me and never letting me down. You are the best mom in the world. You smell like beauty, taste like love, and feel like clouds. Love, Levi.*

We all thrived and our lives may not have looked the way any of us had planned, but I became a mother who shines from within, once again. Many years ago, when I was brand new sober, months away from my suicide, I was told that it was up to me to always find the gifts in every situation, that finding those gifts would be my salvation. These are my thank-yous to those gifts that came from my renaissance.

To the kid on my street who called my son a nerd,

You called my sensitive middle son a nerd. He was walking up to play kickball with you and the rest of

the boys on our street. He was wearing his glasses.
You knew that he's legally blind without his glasses.
You knew that he rarely comes out to play with
you guys, and even so, you made him feel awful.
Thank you and thank all the kids on all the streets
and playgrounds all over the world who make fun
of those of us who look different because it leads
to the kind of conversations that follow between a
parent and a child. I was able to validate him and
tell him that, "Yes, words are powerful and can
hurt, but you can make a difference in the world
by just using the right words." I promise you that
my son will remember you for the rest of his life
like I still remember the kids who made fun of
me. But my son has a choice. He can stand up for
himself, use his voice, and come back to the truth
which hangs on our wall: "There are two kinds of
business: my business and none of my business."
He hears it all the time. What anyone thinks of you
is not your business. The truth is that we are perfect
children of God. As Michelle Obama said, "When
they go low, we go high." I also reminded him that
if he keeps at martial arts, he will be able to protect
himself against any bully that comes his way.

Chapter 62:

Lemons and Lemonade

When Keith and I were going through the hell of our divorce, we went to a tattoo shop to get the words "North Star" inked as our reminder. It would be Keith's first, and I imagine only, tattoo. The idea was it should be ever-present when we are struggling with co-parenting and the emotional complexity of blending families. We were innocent, tired, and had no experience being divorced with children. Our hearts were in the right place, but one cannot predict how life will unfold.

What I can say is that we do an excellent job at showing up for our kids. We are at every game we can be at, and we often sit together, so our boys don't have to look in two separate places for their parents' faces. We are supportive and flexible when we forget goggles, retainers, and lunches, and because we live so close, we do our best to help each other out.

About four years into our separation, we hit a pothole when it came to the North Star plan. Our boys wanted a night once a year where they could just be with their parents at a birthday dinner. No significant others and no extra step-siblings, just their mom, dad, and brothers. To me, this felt like a no-brainer. The boys had to deal with the back and forth of accommodating this new life and sharing their time with lots of new people. They actually really enjoyed it for the most part, but they were vocal about wanting this time to just be with their parents, the original members of the group.

This did not work because Keith's partner came to the story of divorce with a completely different perspective. Having pizza and ice cream after a baseball game wasn't going to happen. Feelings were involved and our open and integrative co-parenting relationship wasn't for everyone. After a grueling and painful session of mediation, the truth washed over me with so much clarity. We were not going to have the kind of divorce story I wanted, but we would have one that gave our boys so much space to not feel the emotional garbage of adulthood. They would get to see both of their parents at school events, sporting games, celebrations, and certain holidays like 4th of July and Halloween. They would never have to worry that there would be tension in the room if Mom and Dad were together. The two of us knew how to show up and put anything standing in our way to the side.

To me, this new truth felt like another divorce. It felt like I had to come to terms with more loss. It would mean less time and fewer new memories with my boys. But divorce is a beast that carries sharp broken glass pieces and discarded garbage with her from everyone in her path. I can only control what I can control, and that is the kind of mother I will be.

I might not have a fantastic 401(k), portfolio, or a career that sparks joy in my heart, but I raise these three humans in a way that inspires and fulfills me. And they get to witness a love story between Jonathan and their mom that will hopefully give them a good example of a healthy, loving relationship. I still hold onto the hope that when the boys are all grown up, we can all sit down to the Thanksgiving table together. I want that, and I welcome it.

Dear Franklin,

I get to be your mother. Until you, I never felt true and uncompromising love. No one prepared me for how intense it would feel. How when you first came home, I would stare at you, willing you to breathe. When I had Elijah, I was terrified by how it would change our relationship. How as you kept getting bigger, I was afraid I would miss each age and want the baby Franklin back. But life is wild and fast and each version of you that you became made me fall more in love with you. I don't miss baby Franklin because the Franklin you are today is one of my all-time favorite humans. You are not the way you are because of me or genetics or anything other than your light and magic. You are a delight to parent. Most days, you're more responsible and mindful than I am. You are kind and loving, but you also caught my family's sarcasm and mischievous nature. Mixing your sweet gentle ways with our inappropriateness and dry sense of humor makes a mother proud. You are the secret penis drawer on foggy windows and mirrors. You like to sing-song whine when the hormones of teenage life are too much. Especially since you know how to read your audience and would never do so in a place that wasn't kosher. I love watching you become a meenager. I hope to honor your need for independence and solitude while I also continue to monitor your phone. But know this, my firstborn, I would choose you in a heartbeat, every time. Even if you weren't my son, I would choose to be near you because I love your soul. And you have

SECONDS AND INCHES · A MEMOIR

excellent taste in the classics (Beastie Boys, Pearl Jam, and Nirvana make a mother proud). Thank you for changing my heart, my life, and this world. It is an honor to be your mother.

Dear Elijah,

When I was pregnant with you, your brother was only a year old, and I couldn't fathom how I would have enough love to give to another baby. I couldn't imagine how incredible it would feel to love you until I finally got to hold you after you were released from the NICU. We were alone in the room, and I touched the palm of your hand. It spread open like a little starfish, and your love washed over me. You taught me how different children can be from their siblings. You came into this world with a fierce personality and the capacity to emotionally detonate when you became anxious. Your intensity brought me to my knees and also gave me the opportunity to learn how to advocate for my child. You have taught me how to love you as you needed to be loved. You have taught me how to use my voice calmly and how to trick you into forgetting about being upset by asking you math problems. I will never forget sitting with you after we told you about the divorce and I introduced the idea of Jonathan in my life. In between mouthfuls of edamame, you told me that you just wanted me to be happy. Your capabilities amaze me: to follow directions, to build massive structures, to build coin sorters and chess boards out of LEGOs. You blow me away with your love for animals and your understanding of existential heartbreak. I knew it when we read *Tuesdays with Morrie* and you got why it made me cry. I love our special snuggle nights, when you sleep in my bed and hold my hand. I love your silly voices and your matter-of-fact answers. Thank you for your twenty-second hugs. I am a better human because you are my son.

Dear Levi,

There are not enough words to explain the gratitude I have for you. When you took your last bath as an eight-year-old, I told you that I would make sure to spend every single birthday with you I could because there was a time when I didn't know if we would get to celebrate your first. You are my karma baby and the loudest human I have ever met. You are inappropriate, potty-mouthed, sarcastic, dramatic, and exhausting. You are glitter and penises. You are darkness and hormones. You take me to my lowest lows and my highest highs. You have molded me into a mother I am proud to be. You have given me lessons that aren't taught in even the best universities. Thank you for being my great teacher and my ball of light, energy, and sass. Thank you for helping me to unfold, trust, rethink, and stretch. Thank you for telling me I'm not being nice when I need to look at my behavior. Thank you for being willing to come back to me after your hormones take over, apologize, hug me, and tell me that your heart doesn't want to be mean. Thank you for feeling safe enough with me to share your fears. Thank you for the past nine years of seeing the world through the eyes of a child who has seen things children should never have to see. Thank you for sharing your massive empathetic soul with us all. May I never forget how lucky I am to be your mother.

Epilogue

I sit in the room, but it is quiet here now. The fire has cleaned and clarified me. The only smoke comes from my incense holder and all that covers the ground are balled up and discarded socks from my boys, my sweet rescue lab, Monroe, and muddied cleats. The walls are covered with pictures and poems and inspirational signs. The couch is old, but clean and comfortable. The door to the hallway is open, so I can feel the breeze from God. And in the hallway, I have laid down a beautiful vintage runner so the passageway between God and myself is soft to travel. In the hallway is nothing. Only signs reminding me to mind my business, and photos showing my beautiful life.

Every day, I find someone or something in the hallway. Ex-husband, bills, medical fears, parenting guilt, overscheduled life, missing Jonathan. But when I can't feel God and when it starts to get too loud or hot, I get off the couch and clear away whatever is blocking me.

I need reminders every day. I forget all the time. I walk on the balance beam, and I hesitate to take the next step. And I feel God's strong hand and hear God's clear voice. "I've got you." And I take another slow and careful step and then I pause and wait and look back. And I feel God's hand and I hear God's voice. "I've got you." I never fail to forget. And God never loses patience.

Dear God,

Thank you for wanting more for me than I could
possibly fathom nineteen years ago, when I signed
myself out of the ICU against medical advice and
walked the one and a half miles home in the winter
morning. You gave me the greatest gift: the gift of
desperation. You were with me on the bathroom
floor. You told me to ask for help. You were with
me on that walk home when I couldn't think of one
more plan. You have been with me every moment
for the last nineteen years, even when I couldn't
feel you or hear you. Thank you for what you have
done with that broken, dying, absent girl. Thank
you for my parents who led the way. Thank you
for the teachers, examples, opportunities, and
gifts. Thank you for saying no, and yes, and wait.
Thank you for the reminders and signs that you
place everywhere for me to see you. Thank you
for the opportunity to be a sober mother to three
little men who would not have a sober mother if
I had been given what I thought I wanted. Thank
you for my ex, who co-parents those boys with me.
Thank you for the true, die-hard friends, and for
the women to work with in recovery. Thank you
for my soul mate who sees me for who I am and
loves me as I am. Thank you for walking with me
in the darkest of hours. Everything since that night
I attempted suicide has been bonus time. I forget
that often. Thank you for the heart you helped
heal and the voice you help me use. I want to do so
much more to show you my gratitude. Please use
me.

Dear Carly,

There is a picture of you on the couch in first grade reading to a doll. When I look at it, I remember how alone you felt, even back then. I see another picture of you getting ready for a dance with hatred in your eyes. You hated how you looked and punished yourself for never being skinny enough. You tortured yourself for so long. You almost didn't make it. I thank God every day you didn't get what you wanted on that bathroom floor in Athens, Ohio. Through it all, through sobriety and college, family and friends, kids and divorce, love and fear, you have learned life's greatest lesson, William Shakespeare's words, which you have tattooed on your wrists: "To thine own self be true." You can finally say that you have come as close to this ideal as you can. Thank you for finally listening to the soul voice within. Thank you for being willing to let go of all that was no longer serving you, no matter how good it made you look on the outside. Thank you for being the amazing mother that you are to those three boys. Because of all the work you do and the time you put in, you are going to raise three conscious, mindful, awake human beings who will carry with them all you have taught them. Thank you for being willing to forgive and to surrender. You are one of my favorite humans on earth. It is not BS that you must get to the place where you can love yourself on your own in order to have a healthy relationship; it's true, and you get to have the most beautiful relationship now because you did the work to love yourself. Please never stop growing, stretching, speaking out, falling down, fucking up, and living because you only get one life. You get just one turn here, and this round is a bonus round from God.

Chapter 63:

Perfect Child of God

What I have discovered in my twenty years of sobriety and nearly forty years on this planet is that I have unimaginable power within me. I feel like a badass, sparkly, lit-up, on fire, brutally honest, potty-mouthed, tattooed woman. I unapologetically stand here and make mistakes, get rid of what no longer works, and do my best to make the small space I live in better because I am in it. This is all bonus time.

With this strength and advocacy comes great responsibility as the mother of these three little men, who would not even be alive if I had gotten what I wanted on January 26, 1999. It is only by seconds and inches that I get to tell my story. That I get to be a mother to these three boys. That I get to fall in love. That I get to show up for others.

If I measured my worth by other people's opinions of me, I would be hiding under a rock. But I'm not because their opinions aren't my business. One of the lessons I have learned along the way is that everybody has a story. Who am I to judge? Life is not a race. There are no prizes for the maximum number of laundry loads completed and dishwashers loaded and unloaded. This is my life. I only get this very short and precious life. What am I going to do with it? When I slow down enough, I remember my truth. I am a perfect child of God, and there's absolutely nothing I can do to change that title. I have nothing to prove. I need no approval. I am enough. I am a soul. This is my body. This is my life. This is the truth for all of us. What are we going to do with our one precious life?

My friend, Sarah, often reminds me that my only business is to behave. Behave and take care of my boys. Be kind and walk with dignity. So I walk this long, uncertain, uneven path. The only way out is through. In the darkness, I have found gifts and dazzling light.

There is one person who is guaranteed to be by my side until the end. She has been there from the beginning. She has not always been treated right, and she has not always been taken care of, but now is the time to come back to her. Love her, heal her, befriend her, and hold her hand. Chin up. Smile at that reflection in the mirror.

Climbing the Willis Tower taught me a valuable lesson. That beast was 103 floors, and while I was known to pound the StairMaster on a daily basis, I had never climbed 103 actual floors. When I reached the fourth floor and saw the big number "4" on the wall, I panicked and started calculating how many more floors I needed to climb. How the hell was I going to do this? Then I reminded myself that what floor I was on was none of my business. It didn't matter when I got to the top because I was not going to quit climbing until I got there. I decided between floors four and five that I would not look up at the wall to see what floor I was on. That I would actually look away from the floor number and just concentrate on my feet, the music, and my breath.

Eventually, I made it to the top. I knew I'd made it because I saw the light coming through the windows and I heard the screaming and the cowbells. When I focus on my life as I focused on climbing that stairwell, without constantly monitoring the floor number, I can do anything.

That is how I went about the business of falling in love with myself, mascara stains under my eyes and all. It is how I face myself in the mirror each day with a smile, love, and acceptance. How can I teach my kids to do that if I can't do it for myself?

Because I loved my daily task of posting thank-yous, and because people were telling me that I was not allowed to stop writing my posts, I decided to set a new goal for myself when my year was up. During the next year, I would post a lesson each day I found within a struggle I experienced that day.

Long ago, there was an incredible woman named Ro Eugene who taught me that in order to do "hard," I needed to search for a lesson in the middle of the struggle. She shared that when one of her five children left their bath running and the ceiling in the kitchen began to rain, instead of yelling at them or feeling bad for herself, she thought, "Thank God I have all these old towels to help me clean up." Her willingness to find the lessons and gifts has helped transform me into a woman who automatically looks for the gift or lesson in all the growth opportunities that come my way. Because of her and so many others along this path, I can't walk this earth without seeing the gifts, lessons, and perspective.

Chapter 64:

Lessons

Here are a few of the lessons I have found, in each day, as I have embarked on this next commitment.

Lesson: Put on your own oxygen mask first.

I sat next to my guru baby, burning up and snoring, and thought of what they say on the plane before takeoff: "In case of a cabin pressure emergency, put on your own mask first before assisting others." Until the plane is actually nosediving and the masks drop from the ceiling, you don't know if you would put your own mask on before getting one on your child's face. It sounds reasonable, but it isn't. When you're a parent, it is nearly impossible. Levi is mostly healthy now. With the weekly injections I give him to stop his immune system from flaring and spiking fevers above 107, he is just a regular kid running around, being inappropriate, fighting with his brothers, being dramatic, and kicking soccer balls. But when a flare hits, he is motionless, limp, and curled in the fetal position. We can't always make the flares better. Sometimes our job is to put his mask on, get him settled, and grab our masks with the other hand. When it is time to give him the painful shot that he begs me not to give him, I tell him I have to. Reluctantly and weepily, he assents. I give him the shot, it hurts, and then it makes him better. Today's lesson is that, sometimes, we have to go through pain to heal. As a parent, of course I wish I could protect my kids from pain, but sometimes, that's not an option. And I don't want to rob them of their lessons. The only way out is through.

Lesson: Never give up on those we love.

As Jonathan and I sat and watched the sun set at a beautiful plaza in Lisbon, I opened up a card that my mom gave me before our trip. Because of all the work she had done and the mother she became, she was still giving me these gift package cards with her heart poured into that blue Bic pen. Because I love her deeply and also because she hurt me in a way that sliced me open and forced me to find my own approval during my divorce, opening up her card on my honeymoon in Portugal was a gift worth more than she would ever know. In the letter were words I had long ago given up hope of hearing. I was filled with overwhelming gratitude as I read the words that melted the last icicles around my heart. She knew I was happy with Jonathan and that I made the right choice for me. My happiness made her happy. Just like my misery had made her miserable. This is the life of loving someone so deeply. Part of this journey is accepting that not everyone we love will agree with our choices, and sometimes, we have to take those lonely steps without the approval of those we love.

It can be frightening, but it can also be a gift because it forces us to be so unbelievably certain that the choices we are making are right for us.

I discovered that my mom was able to see and know, in her own time, that my path was perfect for me. While I no longer needed those words of approval, hearing them was like a second skin healing over a bad scar. Where it was once broken, it is now stronger. The lesson today is to never give up on those we love, because everyone gets to where they get to, in their own time.

Lesson: Grow up and behave.

So many "nevers" have happened in my life today. I sat in a pizza shop in Madison, Ohio, between my husband Jonathan and my ex-husband Keith. We were all in Madison watching Franklin in a soccer tournament. Because of doing a ton of work and taking a lot of high roads, we are at a place where we can sit at a tiny table in a pizza shop and coexist peacefully. Lulu's parents were divorced when she was an adult, and she told me horror stories of not being able to be at any holiday with both her parents present. How they would disparage and judge each other. The struggle of managing these worlds is real, but the truth is (except in rare cases when dealing with someone who is emotionally or mentally ill) not making it work and not being able to sit at a tiny table together in a pizza shop is only impossible for those unwilling to grow up and be an adult. Today's lesson is to grow up and behave. Just like they taught us in kindergarten: be kind and treat others how you want to be treated. Maybe one day, my blended family dream (with all of our kiddos grown up and with loved ones of their own coming back to a massive table with tons of us, all sitting together, laughing and doing our best) will be a reality because we are all willing to sit down together and behave.

Lesson: A plan means a chance.

No matter how hard I try to look at the facts logically when I go to the NIH with Levi, my body always responds with anxiety. My belly gets tight, and I get nauseous with worry that they'll tell us they're done looking at Levi. That they can't figure out what's wrong with him, and he doesn't match anything they're researching. But that's never happened in six years. And then I sit in the waiting room, and I see a boy in a wheelchair who is almost completely paralyzed. I see a twelve-year-old girl who won't sit still to watch a show on the phone but, instead, tries to hit the aquarium and her mom. Then Levi and I spend hours in our little room getting bloodwork while nine doctors explain the next plan. And there's my lesson. We have a plan. We have a team. We have what we need. I'll never forget the afternoon I met another mom in the computer lounge at Boston

Children's. Her son was the same age as Levi and we exchanged tired grins. I asked her when she was going home, and she said soon. I told her she was so lucky, and then she told me she was bringing her son home to die. Today's lesson is to remember that if we have a plan, we have a chance. A plan means there's a future. A future means there are options. And options mean there can be attitude changes, objectivity, and space. We get to try a new plan. How lucky am I?

Lesson: Allow the hard times to strengthen you so you can hold others up.

Nine years ago, Levi was sedated for an angiogram at Boston Children's Hospital to see if his head's venous system was sufficient or if he would need to undergo multiple brain surgeries. Before going to Boston, Chapman reminded me that I was on a mission to save my baby boy and that there was no time for emotions. Eleanor Roosevelt said, "A woman is like a tea bag; you can't tell how strong she is until you put her in hot water." I can assure you that I did not feel strong that day and that I could not stop the emotions. I was exhausted, angry, and terrified that I may have to board a plane back to Cleveland without my youngest son. Today's lesson is to allow our excruciating moments to make us stronger, so we can hold others up when they're in their hot water. Not a day goes by where I don't thank the universe for the cards we were dealt. One of my friends is currently in hell. She is dealing with her child's complex medical issues, and her entire life is up in the air. I don't talk very often about what happens to a parent when they are in fear for their child's life. I like to focus on the positives and not drag others down with how dark it can get. But I have my own PTSD from some of the sights I've seen as Levi's mother. I can't see a clock or a number on an exercise machine with a 106 or 107 and not see the numbers on the thermometer. When I'm not with Levi and my phone rings, my first thought is, *It happened.* Jonathan watched his daughter take her last breath. Kevin held his daughter in his arms in the middle of the street. These experiences change us. They scar us, but they do not ruin us. I am better off for what I understand. I am a better mother because of the emergency rooms and waiting rooms I have sat in. I am a better human because I know what to say and not say to those going through hell. Today's lesson is to realize that our scars give us strength and the understanding we need to help others face their own challenges. Today, I am beholden to my scars.

Lesson: To be in a partnership that inspires your children.

I was listening to Oprah's *SuperSoul Sunday* and the guest was asked how he raised his three sons to be good men. He told Oprah the most important thing he did for his sons was to love their mother and treat her like she was the most important person in the universe. My throat bulged with emotion. I was married to Keith at the time. I had a good marriage on paper, but could I have said that our sons saw us treat each other that way? No, I couldn't. There were many other reasons we didn't make it, but that was one of the questions that really bothered my soul. What would my boys grow up believing about how a man should treat a woman? What would they see in their own home? Would they know how to romance, lift up, and be there for their partners the way all of us dream of? This was one of the soul questions I had to face. I made some pretty difficult decisions years ago that placed my three sons in the position to see a love story in front of their eyes. To see a man who looks at a woman as if she is his queen. They get to see love letters in the mail to their mom. Today's lesson is to make sure I am living a love story that inspires my children. Because they'll either want to repeat or run from what they see. (This is not to say that those who raise their children alone are doing anything wrong. I was willing to do it alone if it meant they wouldn't grow up with a skewed perception of love.)

Lesson: You are blessed. Never ever forget that.

It is so easy to forget that we are blessed, between the fighting, whining, homework, attitudes, endless eating, crumbs, socks, all of it. I am not a morbid person, but I do live with the daily reminder that I am blessed to have these children, to be their mother, to pick them up from practice, to help them with their word studies. I clicked on a post about a father's list of ten lessons

he's learned since losing his son. I always click
on these kinds of stories. Because I've come so
close, I'm surrounded by people who have lost
a child, and there is not a single part of me that
ever wants to forget that I am so fortunate to
have my boys. I fall short every day. I don't only
worry about my kid with medical conditions. I
worry about all of them. Our lives can change in
an instant, by walking across the street, biking
down the sidewalk, going to school, playing on
the playground, or running on the soccer field.
Some say reading these stories makes me too
focused on the worst that could happen when I
should be imagining better outcomes. But I see
it differently. I use this father's list of ten lessons
he learned, and all the other stories I can get my
hands on as my defense against complaining. The
tantrums, the Chewy bar wrappers, the endless
laundry, the driving all over the place. They are
all gifts. I am blessed. I get to do all of it. One of
my best friends never gets to tell his daughter to
clean her room, ever again. My husband never gets
to give his daughter a bath, ever again. My dear
friend never gets to have a Nerf fight with his son,
ever again. My grandmother never got to throw
a birthday party for her daughter, ever again.
Today's lesson is to remember that you're blessed.

Lesson: Must love self as is.

I was sitting on the floor in our hotel room
looking into the mirror. We were in Lisbon
for our honeymoon. A memory came to me

of a young lady who landed in Nice, France seventeen years earlier. She didn't know a soul, could hardly stand herself, and needed to make peace with herself as she was. On that night in France, I remember crying, laughing, and talking to myself in the mirror. I discovered then that I am all I have, and I better learn to love myself, or I'm screwed. Fast forward to Lisbon, I saw my husband be uncomfortable in the role of tourist, embarrassed to take selfies in front of ancient buildings, and wanting to not stick out so much. I felt so much gratitude that I not only didn't care what I looked like here or anywhere, but that I celebrate who I am. This lesson is not a given; it is earned. I thank the universe for my riches.

Lesson: Rock bottom can become the solid foundation on which we can rebuild our lives.

My twentieth sober anniversary was surreal. So much love came my way. I told Jonathan that it's kind of incredible that I celebrate this day because this day twenty years ago was the shittiest day of my life. It was January 27, 1999, and I had just signed myself out against medical advice and walked home from the hospital in shorts in the middle of winter. I was spiritually bankrupt in a way I could not fathom recovering from. I was humiliated, broken, and without the only tool I had to numb it all. I was not relieved to be alive, and I could not see a life that was worth living. I was tired and without plans. A line in my sobriety guidebook says, "To be doomed to an alcoholic death or to live on a spiritual basis

are not always easy alternatives to face." This line
sounds ridiculous to anyone who hasn't placed
themselves in this position. To the outsider, it's a
no-brainer. But to me, it was pure torture. Today's
lesson is to remember that while some days feel
painful, exhausting, and dark, it is always possible
to look upon that day with new eyes. This lesson is
exemplified in one of JK Rowling's famous words,
"Rock bottom became the solid foundation on
which I rebuilt my life."

THE END

ACKNOWLEDGMENTS

Here we go, please know this, I will forget someone I really want to remember, just like I forget my phone and keys. It is not intentional, and I love you even if I didn't mention your name.

Firstly, I want to thank the women and men in church basements all over the world who welcomed this mess of a human and sat next to me while I shook and cried and sweated all over the place. I would be nothing if it wasn't for your kindness, examples, and patience.

Elizabeth, who I only know as "El": If you hadn't reached out to me, offering me one of the greatest opportunities of my life, this book would still be just a dream in my mind. And then, you took my little sweet thank-yous and told me you wanted more. That you wanted the real stories behind the thank-yous. And then you kept pushing me and believing in me. And your belief made it all a reality. I am honored to be a part of Jaded Ibis Press. I love you then and now and always. I am rooting for you.

To Jen, I am not a crier. But when I read the words you wrote for my foreword, I bawled, multiple times. When I first heard your story, I felt like I finally found my missing sister. And your strength and life has given me permission to live mine. Thank you for saying, "yes," to my book and thank you for seeing in it what you saw. I love you.

Thank you to all the writers and thought leaders who took the time to read this book and offer brilliant words about it.

For my Shaker Heights village of moms and dads and neighbors and kindness. Moving to your hood has made our lives infinitely better, and I am proud to be a member of this giving community. I cannot do this on my own. The carpooling and friendship and support.

For all the people who commented or liked or sent me private messages about how my writing made them feel. For my podcast listeners. All of you, whether you know it or not, made me believe in myself.

For the women who allow me to walk by their side: I am humbled and grateful and I hold your secrets in my vault, and you liberate me with each piece of honesty you lay at my feet. And for Nicky, seventeen miles in and seventeen miles out.

My lady friends: Allyson and Elana for telling me I lost my light, reading early drafts, and always having my back. Heather for being my divorced friend so I don't feel all alone in this world. The women I have connected with through my writing and mutual badassery, especially, Kristie and Jessica. Erin for being the kind of woman who comes to you with the truth and then meets you decades later and becomes one of your mama bears. Jasmine and Kathryn who sat me down and consistently told me the truth as they saw it. My work sisters, who deal with me all week and laugh and don't judge me too hard when I have an adult tantrum. "But did you die?"

Kevin, for all you have taught me, for making me into a woman who has a voice and for sharing your endless grief with me. Your beautiful baby girl is never going to leave your side.

Sarah, for sitting next to me on the picnic bench and never judging me. For telling me that one day none of my drama would matter anymore. For being the coolest, strongest, ride or die mama in my life.

My family for being so close and supportive and sarcastic. I am one lucky girl to be part of this crew. For my parents who endlessly support me and my boys. For getting sober and changing all of our lives. For my mom and Lulu, who read every single draft of this book. For your strength and love. For Lulu and Papa, who walked away from a living hell and created an empire of humans out of nothing, your history and pain have given birth to new generations who will never forget.

My three boys: You are my universe. I am whole because of your love. You are my teachers, my dharma, my life's work. Thank you for the laughter, the penises, the growth opportunities, for molding me into an advocate and the mother I always wanted to be. Your forever home is in my heart. And I promise I will work day and night to ensure you never know what it is like to feel unsafe.

To the love of my life, Jonathan. You came in and changed everything. You are my favorite person and my confidante. I am a better human because of your love. I thank you for your endless support and for reminding me when I need to, "Calm the f down," and for holding my hand in the waves.

CPSIA information can be obtained
at www.ICGtesting.com
Printed in the USA
LVHW040438210920
666619LV00004B/202

9 781938 841118